# Jehovah's Witnesses, Jesus Christ, and the Gospel of John

*Dr. ... Solomansen*
*3-3-89*

# Jehovah's Witnesses, Jesus Christ, and the Gospel of John

Robert M. Bowman, Jr.

**BAKER BOOK HOUSE**

Grand Rapids, Michigan 49516

Copyright 1989 by Baker Book House Company

Printed in the United States of America

**Library of Congress Cataloging in Publication Data**

Bowman, Robert M.
 Jehovah's Witnesses, Jesus Christ, and the Gospel of
John.

 Bibliography: p.
 Includes index.
 1. Bible. N.T. John I, 1—Criticism, interpretation,
etc. 2. Bible. N.T. John VIII, 58-Criticism, interpretation, etc. 3. Jesus Christ—History of doctrines—
Early church, ca. 30-600. 4. Jehovah's Witnesses—Controversial literature. I. Title.
 BS2615.2.B66  1988    226'.506'088289    88-34319
 ISBN 0-8010-0955-3

# Contents

# Foreword

A considerable amount of material has been written on the subject of Jehovah's Witnesses and their mishandling of biblical texts, particularly about their consistent abuse of the rules of grammar and context where the Jehovah's Witnesses' *New World Translation* is concerned. Unfortunately, most of this material has been written by scholars who are not thorough students of the cults in general nor of Jehovah's Witnesses in particular. Readers are often confused and overwhelmed by a mass of material which they do not have either the vocabulary or scholastic background to understand.

In this succinct yet detailed volume Robert Bowman has brought together both scholarly information and experiential insight, and the reader can clearly see the errors of Watchtower thinking.

Quite apart from numerous interviews with Jehovah's Witnesses and careful study of their literature, including the *New World Translation* of the Bible, Mr. Bowman has worked for the past four years at Christian Research Institute specializing in the analysis of cultic writings, and has authored numerous papers and articles and written countless letters to people confused by the cults. He is informed, scholarly, and exacting in his analysis of John 1:1, 8:58, and 20:28, and Jehovah's Witnesses' misuse of scholarly sources to bolster their false doctrines.

Of real interest to the reader will be Mr. Bowman's exposure of the Watchtower's unwillingness to admit mistakes, and their distortion and misuse of recognized scholarship in an attempt to justify their denial of the trinity and the deity of Jesus Christ.

The dearth of well-written and readable material on the Watchtower's abuse of the texts, especially those in the Gospel of John, has been alleviated with the publication of this book. Careful students of the Bible, scholars as well as laymen, will profit from the extensive research Mr. Bowman has utilized and presented in a readable and practical form.

This volume for some time to come will be a standard reference in this particular area of cultic theology. It is a delight to recommend its usage to the Christian public and interested scholars everywhere.

Walter Martin
San Juan Capistrano, California
February 1, 1988

# Acknowledgments

My thinking on the issues discussed in this book has been deepened and, hopefully, matured by dialogue with other Christians. I am especially grateful to Earl Stewart who spent countless hours in conversation with me, provided numerous references to scholarly books and articles of relevance, and made specific suggestions concerning this book.

I would also like to thank Dr. Walter Martin, director of Christian Research Institute, for the opportunity to serve with him since 1984 in CRI's vital ministry of giving Christians reasons for faith and answers to the many cultic and heretical abuses of Scripture circulating today. Dr. Martin's writings on the Jehovah's Witnesses stimulated my early thinking on John 1:1 and 8:58. I am also grateful to Dr. Martin for writing the Foreword to this book.

Finally, a special word of gratitude goes to my wife Cathy for the hundreds of hours she spent as a "scholar's widow" while I researched and wrote this book. Without her patient support this book might never have been written.

# Introduction

The controversial translation of John 1:1 in the Jehovah's Witnesses' *New World Translation* (NWT) is well known: "In [the] beginning the Word was, and the Word was with God, and the Word was a god." Almost as well known is their rendering of John 8:58, according to which Jesus said, "Before Abraham came into existence, I have been."

These renderings with their accompanying interpretation have been discussed by biblical scholars and evangelical apologists many times, and scholarly treatments of their meaning can be found in many commentaries and in several scholarly articles. Yet there is need for further analysis of the NWT renderings and the arguments used by the Jehovah's Witnesses (hereafter abbreviated "JWs" for brevity's sake) to defend their unorthodox interpretation of these verses.

One reason why a new critique is necessary is that the JWs continue to cite newer scholarly sources in defense of their interpretation. For example, in recent years they appealed to the fine article on Mark 15:39 and John 1:1 by Philip B. Harner in the 1973 *Journal of Biblical Literature*[1] in defense of their rendering of John 1:1. On John 8:58, they have refined their argument by appealing to the Greek idiom known as the "present of past action in progress," which a few scholars have said could be found in John 8:58.

Another reason for a thorough discussion of these texts in

relation to the JWs is the increasing influence of Nelson Herle, a JW in Los Angeles. Calling himself a "self-made expert on the Trinity," he has distributed hundreds of copies of his unpublished manuscript *The Trinity Doctrine Examined in the Light of History and the Bible*.[2] In this manuscript he discusses both John 1:1 and 8:58 at length. The influence of his work is best seen in the fact (documented further in this book) that his treatment of these two verses appears to have redirected the Watchtower Society's own apologetic for their interpretation of the texts.

It must also be said that most discussions of the texts either ignore the JWs' arguments, or narrowly focus only on refuting the JWs and thus fail to put the matter in its broader context. This study, though not definitive or exhaustive, seeks to remedy this lack.

The specific purpose of this book is to show not only that the JW interpretation of John 1:1 and 8:58 is in error, but also to show that the trinitarian interpretation is correct. This book should also be useful, therefore, to persons who are interested in the interpretation of these texts but in a different connection than with the JWs.

A word must be said about the assumptions under which this study is written. In a nutshell, these assumptions are the inerrant authority of Scripture, the principles of valid reasoning (or logic), and the standard recognized principles of biblical interpretation. Works setting forth the evangelical Christian understanding of the Bible's authority and how it is to be interpreted are available for those who desire background reading on these subjects.[3]

To sort out all of the details of the interpretation of John 1:1 and 8:58 and evaluate the arguments put forth by the JWs for their interpretation, it will be necessary to discuss Greek words, grammar, and syntax (word order). It is hoped that JWs themselves may be helped by this study, as well as those who are seriously considering adopting their teachings. Since most people who are in either of these two categories do not understand Greek or grammatical terms, these things will be carefully explained in a way which, it is hoped, any person fluent in English can understand. Those readers who already understand what various technical terms and concepts mean may wish to skim the sections which explain the more elementary concepts.

JWs reading this study should bear in mind that their own publications discuss Greek words and grammar, notably in relation to these two texts. Indeed, in March 1987 an article appeared in the JW magazine *Awake!* with the title, "How Knowing Greek Led Me to Know God."[4] In this article the author, Nicholas Kip, claimed that knowing Greek before he became a JW helped him to see the truth of their teachings. Interestingly enough, he mentioned as a specific example the JWs' teaching on John 8:58.

Therefore, JWs should not be intimidated by the discussion of Greek words and grammar in this book. At the very least, they should find that things which they previously did not understand will be clarified in this study. Nor is it legitimate for JWs to dismiss the matter by saying that they refuse to "fight over words," since they themselves publish literature disputing the meaning of certain key verses in the Bible.

In this book I have sought to consider fairly and honestly all of the arguments put forth by JWs in their publications in defense of their interpretation of John 1:1 and 8:58. I have spent many hours in dialogue with JWs, including Nelson Herle and several other JWs who profess to have a working knowledge of Greek and Hebrew. I have gone to great lengths to give the JWs every chance to defend their position. In the summer of 1984 I submitted to several of these JWs a 15-page paper on John 8:58 and asked for their criticisms. I received very little in the way of substantive criticisms of my major points. In April 1987 I wrote to Nicholas Kip in response to his article in *Awake!*, and asked him if he would be willing to dialogue with me on John 8:58 and other matters. Kip refused, referring to such a dialogue as "fighting over words"—which is truly ironic, since in the

*Awake!* article he claims to have joined the JWs because he thought they were right about the meaning of certain biblical words.

Then in October, 1987, I wrote to Nicholas Kip, Nelson Herle, and the Watchtower Bible and Tract Society (see Appendix D), informing them of this book. In these letters I invited any interested JW to write a rebuttal to the book, to be included in the book as an appendix. Not one person responded to this invitation.

Inevitably questions will be asked about the author. I am an evangelical Christian, and regard the Bible as the only unerring revelation of God's truth. I have never been a JW, and therefore am not an "apostate" by JW standards. I hold a master's degree in biblical studies and theology from Fuller Theological Seminary, a degree requiring competency in biblical Greek and Hebrew. At present I am pursuing a Ph.D. in theology from Westminster Theological Seminary in Philadelphia, while working part-time as an Editorial Consultant for the Christian Research Institute in Southern California, where for over four years I was a researcher and editor. CRI is an evangelical ministry which disseminates information on heretical and non-Christian religions.

Comments, questions, and criticisms of this book are welcome. Please address all correspondence to Robert M. Bowman, Jr., Christian Research Institute, P. O. Box 500, San Juan Capistrano, CA 92693-0500.

# Jesus as God in John 1:1

# 1

## The Eternal Person of the Word

The purpose of this book is to refute the JW interpretation of John 1:1 and 8:58 and to defend the trinitarian interpretation of those texts. It should be recognized, however, that these conflicting interpretations do share some features in common. In this chapter we shall see where JWs and evangelicals agree and disagree about John 1:1, compare the JW interpretation with those of other antitrinitarian sects, and begin our study of the first part of the verse.

### Points of Agreement

Both JWs and trinitarian Christians reject modalistic and unitarian interpretations of both of these texts. *Modalism* is the doctrine that God, who is only one person, manifested himself in the human Jesus Christ, so that in some sense Jesus is God the Father. The JWs agree that God is one person, but deny he was incarnated in Jesus; whereas trinitarians agree that God was incarnated in Jesus, but insist that while there is only one God, that God is more than one person. *Unitarianism* holds that there is only one person who is God, and that Jesus was a mere man who did not preexist his human life and who is not "divine" in any literal sense of the word. While accepting the idea that God is one person, the JWs deny that Jesus was a mere man.

With regard to John 1:1, both JWs and trinitarian Christians agree that Jesus Christ was "the Word" prior to his becoming human. They also both agree, therefore, that the Word was a preexistent living person, not merely an abstraction or idea. Furthermore, they both agree that "the Word was with God" means that the Word—Jesus Christ—existed alongside God the Father as a person distinct from him. Finally, they both agree that in some sense the preexistent Word was divine.

These common understandings should be kept in mind as the differences are discussed.

## How Other Unorthodox Sects Treat John 1:1

It will be instructive to note at the outset that the JWs are not the only new sect ("new" in the sense of originating in the last two centuries) that offers an unusual rewording of this classic prooftext of the deity of Jesus Christ. Joseph Smith, the founder of Mormonism, prepared an *Inspired Version* of the Bible in which John 1:1 was changed to read:

> In the beginning was the gospel preached through the Son. And the gospel was the word, and the word was with the Son, and the Son was with God, and the Son was of God.[1]

Victor Paul Wierwille, the founder of The Way International, offered an expanded translation of John 1:1 that distinguished between "the Word" as another name for God and "the revealed Word" which was Jesus Christ and which existed "in the beginning" only in the foreknowledge of God:

> In the beginning was the Word (God), and the (revealed) Word was with *(pros)* God (with Him in His foreknowledge, yet independent of Him), and the Word was God.[2]

Even those unorthodox sects which do not retranslate John 1:1 reinterpret it to fit their various views about the person of Christ. Herbert W. Armstrong, the founder of the Worldwide Church of God, agreed that Jesus was "God," but went on to argue that human beings have the opportunity to become "God" (or a part of the "God family") as well.[3] Mary Baker Eddy, the founder of Christian Science, understood John 1:1 to mean "The Christ-healing was . . . practised even before the Christian era . . ."[4] and also commented on it, ". . . This great truth of God's impersonality and individuality and of man in His image and likeness, individual, but not personal, is the foundation of Christian Science. . . ."[5] Various teachers in the United Pentecostal Church and other Oneness Pentecostal bodies, which hold a modalistic view of Christ, interpret John 1:1 to mean that God's "Plan" (their interpretation of *logos*, generally translated "Word") to become a man in Jesus was in God's mind from the beginning.[6]

Because these sects are all antitrinitarian, they have found it necessary to come up with novel interpretations of such texts as John 1:1. Some of them have even attempted to back up their interpretations with analysis of the Greek text, notably The Way International and the Oneness Pentecostals. However, none of these sects have devoted the attention to John 1:1 given it by the JWs. Nor has any other antitrinitarian sect been as successful as the JWs in passing off their interpretation of John 1:1 as a scholarly based alternative to the trinitarian interpretation. This is why the JWs' interpretation of John 1:1 is especially deserving of careful analysis and refutation from an orthodox perspective.

## Same Text, Conflicting Interpretations

Because our discussion of John 1:1 will be paying extremely close attention to the actual words of the text, it will be helpful to set out here the Greek text in transliterated form, with a word for word rendering underneath. There is no disagreement between JWs and orthodox Christians as to the text of John's opening verse.[7]

| *en archē ēn ho logos* | (Clause A) |
|---|---|
| IN BEGINNING WAS THE WORD | |
| *kai ho logos ēn pros ton theon* | (Clause B) |
| AND THE WORD WAS WITH THE GOD | |
| *kai theos ēn ho logos* | (Clause C) |
| AND GOD WAS THE WORD | |

The JW interpretation of this text is as follows. *Clause A:* The Word came into existence before the creation of the physical universe as a mighty angelic being, the first and only direct creation of Jehovah God. He was not eternal. *Clause B:* The Word existed alongside Jehovah God as a separate entity from God. *Clause C:* The Word was a god, that is, a mighty one, a being wielding great power, specifically a mighty angel, sharing some of God's qualities but only to a lesser degree or extent.

The orthodox, trinitarian interpretation of John 1:1 may be summarized as follows. *Clause A:* The Word was continuing to exist at the beginning of time, and therefore was eternal. *Clause B:* The Word existed alongside the Father as a distinct person, though not a separate entity. *Clause C:* The Word was God in essence, that is, he had the full nature, essence, and attributes of God, though he was not the same person as the Father.

Most critiques of the JW interpretation of John 1:1 focus exclusively on Clause C. Though that clause shall require the most careful attention, it is necessary to examine the first two clauses as well in order to understand John's opening statement as a whole.

## "In the Beginning Was the Word"

The first two words of the Gospel of John, *en archē*, also begin the Book of Genesis in the Septuagint (LXX).[8] Commentators have frequently pointed out this parallel, and have drawn the obvious conclusion that the "beginning" of John 1:1 is the same beginning as that of Genesis 1:1. The

JWs resist this conclusion, however, because they wish to deny that the Word existed "before" the absolute beginning of time, since this would mean that the Word was God. Thus, in their 1984 Reference Edition of the NWT, they do not list Genesis 1:1 as a cross-reference to John 1:1, though three other texts are cross-referenced to the word *beginning* (Prov. 8:22; Col. 1:15; Rev. 3:14).[9]

There does not, however, seem to be any valid reason to deny the connection between the opening words of Genesis and John. JWs sometimes argue that the omission of the definite article in this clause is significant—"in [the] beginning"—but this argument backfires: the LXX rendering of Genesis 1:1 also omits the definite article, and the opening words of Genesis in the NWT read "In [the] beginning" also![10] The only other argument seems to be that the expression *en archē* of itself need not refer to the beginning of time (Acts 11:15; Phil. 4:15).[11] The point is a trivial one, since it is the use of the expression at the beginning of the book in the context of discussing the creation of all things (John 1:3) that makes the expression parallel, not the mere use of the expression considered by itself.

Indeed, the parallels between the two passages are many:

1. The words *en archē* occur at the beginning of each book;
2. The name *God (ho theos)* occurs in the opening sentence in each book, and frequently thereafter as well;
3. Both passages speak about the creation of all things;
4. The name given to the preexistent Christ, "the Word," reminds us of the frequent statement in Genesis, "And God said, 'Let there be . . .'" —that is, in Genesis God creates by speaking the word, in John he creates through the person of the Word;
5. Both passages in Greek use the words *egeneto* ("came into existence"), *phōs* ("light"), and *skotos* or *skotia* ("darkness"), and both contrast light and darkness.

These points of similarity taken together constitute a powerful cumulative case for understanding *en archē* to be referring
to the same beginning in John 1:1 as that of Genesis 1:1—the
beginning of time itself.

It might be helpful here to say something about the
relationship between time and eternity. Some philosophers
and theologians maintain that eternity is simply time with no
beginning and no end, whereas other thinkers hold that eternity is transcendent over time—sometimes called "timeless-
ness," though that is not the most accurate term for it. The
question of the precise relationship between time and eternity
is not explicitly answered in Scripture. The statements in
Hebrews about the creation of the ages (Heb. 1:2; 11:3) suggest
that time itself is created. Scientific evidence for the "big bang"
as the beginning of the universe has recently made it clear that
time and space came into existence together with the creation of
the material universe.[12] For this reason it is best not to view
eternity as merely time without beginning, but rather as a
unique attribute of the transcendent God.

Once it is understood that *en archē* in John 1:1 refers to the
beginning of time, it becomes inescapably clear that John is
asserting that the Word was eternal. To say that the Word *was*
in the beginning is to say the same thing as that the Word
was already existing when time began. If one wishes to think
of eternity as time without any actual beginning or ending,
then one would paraphrase John as meaning that the Word
existed "before" the beginning; or, if one prefers, as does this
writer, to think of time as beginning with the creation of the
space-time universe and of eternity as God's transcendence
over time, then one would paraphrase John as meaning that
the Word's existence transcends time. However the point is
expressed, it is the same: the Word is eternal.

The JWs, of course, find such a conclusion intolerable.
They insist that even if the "beginning" of John 1:1 is the
same as that of Genesis 1:1, that all John means to say is that
the Word existed before the creation of the physical universe.
(Since it appears certain that time began with the creation of

the physical universe, such an admission would logically imply his eternality, but the JWs have evidently not considered this line of reasoning.) They feel sure that all John wanted to say was that the Word has existed *since* the beginning as the first creation of God, but not that the Word was eternal.

Had John wanted to say that the Word was the first creation of God, or even simply say that the Word existed before the rest of creation, there are a number of ways he could have said so clearly and without any possibility of misunderstanding. He could have written, "*From* the beginning," using the word *apo* instead of *en*, as he did repeatedly in his writings in the expression *ap' archēs* (John 8:44; 15:27; 1 John 1:1; 2:7, 13, 14, 24; 3:8, 11; 2 John 5, 6). This would trace his existence back to the beginning without telling us anything about his existence "before" the beginning (if such existence were possible). Or, he could have written, "In the beginning the Word *came into existence*," substituting for the word *ēn* the word *egeneto*, which occurs repeatedly in the Prologue (John 1:3, 6, 10, 14, 17). This would have settled the debate forever in favor of the JW interpretation of the text, since it would be an explicit affirmation of the creation of the preincarnate Jesus. Yet John wrote neither of these things. Instead, he wrote what most naturally would be (and as a matter of historical record has been) interpreted as a declaration of the eternality of the Word. "In the beginning the Word *was*"; the verb *was* is the imperfect past tense verb *ēn*, here unquestionably used of durative, continuing existence. To continue existing at the beginning of time is to be eternal by definition.

In an attempt to escape this line of reasoning, the JW Nelson Herle has cited A. T. Robertson's comment, "Hence we need not insist that *ēn* (Jo. 1:1) is strictly durative always (imperfect). It may be aorist also."[13] (An *aorist* is a past tense verb that denotes a single event or an act at a single point in time, as opposed to an ongoing process or state or condition.) What Herle ignores here is that Robertson himself indicates that while *ēn* is not always durative, in most cases it is, and it certainly is in John 1:1. The reason why it must be regarded as durative is that it occurs not just once in John 1:1a, but several times in a series of statements about the Word (John 1:1abc, 2, 4ab), none of which is aoristic. Moreover, there is a strong and measured contrast in the Prologue (John 1:1–18) between the imperfect *ēn* and the aorist *egeneto,* which proves beyond question that *ēn* in John 1:1 is durative.

Our examination of Clause A of John 1:1, then, leads us to conclude that John very clearly teaches that the Word was eternal. This one statement, however, would not have been sufficient to identify the Word. Is "the Word" simply another name for God? Is the Word merely an attribute of God—his reason, or mind—and nothing more, or is the Word a real person? If he is a real person, is he identical in every sense with God, or is he identical in some sense with God, or is he a separate entity apart from God, though eternal? It is necessary to read and interpret correctly the second and third clauses of John 1:1 to answer these questions properly.

### "And the Word Was with God"

Before discussing the meaning of this statement, a peculiar sideline argument frequently raised by the JWs in this connection ought to be mentioned. It is extremely common for JWs to ask with reference to this text why the Holy Spirit is not mentioned as another person who was also with God. The answer is that John was concerned at that point to write about the Word, not the Holy Spirit. The JWs reason that if the Holy Spirit is not mentioned in John 1:1, then the Holy Spirit either (a) was not there; or (b) was not a person; they opt for the latter explanation. But there is a third explanation: John simply did not care to mention the Holy Spirit at that point. One could just as easily (and mistakenly) argue that because Matthew mentions only two women at Jesus' tomb (Matt. 28:1), that there were only those two women there (*compare* Mark 16:1; Luke 24:10). It is foolish to build opposition to historic orthodox Christian doctrine on such weak arguments from silence.

Next, a brief comment is in order about the spelling of the words for "God" in John 1:1. In Clause B the word is *theon*, whereas in Clause C it is *theos*. Uninformed JWs have often said that the different spellings indicated different meanings for the words. Fortunately, the Watchtower Society has published an official statement admitting that this is not so. As the article correctly noted, ". . . the difference is simply a matter of complying with the Greek grammatical case used."[14] In languages such as Greek, nouns have different endings depending on what function they perform in the sentence. The Greek word for "God," *theos*, can be spelled a variety of ways depending on its grammatical case, as the following sentences illustrate:

"See, the Lamb of *God*" (*theou*; John 1:29 NWT)

"No man has seen *God* at any time" (*theon*; John 1:18a NWT)

"For *God* so loved the world" (*theos*; John 3:16 NWT)

In the above sentences, *theou* is in what is called the genitive case, *theon* is in the accusative case, and *theos* is in the nominative case. "Nominative" refers to the case in which a noun is used either as the subject or to further identify the subject. In the sentence "John, the man you saw, is a teacher," the words *John*, *man*, and *teacher* are all nominative (although only the word *John* is the subject).

There is no need here to discuss the meaning of the term *with* (*pros*), since the JWs (unlike modalists such as the Oneness Pentecostals) recognize that the Word was a person existing alongside the one called "God." What needs to be treated in some depth is the question of how the Word can be with God and yet be God. The most basic Watchtower argument against taking John 1:1 as an affirmation that the Word is Almighty God is that the Word is said in the same verse to be "with God," and obviously no one can be with himself; therefore, the Word cannot be God.[15]

In one respect the JWs are quite right. The Word certainly cannot be with "God" and be "God" unless the term *God* somehow changes significance from the first to the second usage. The question is what sort of shift in nuance is to be inferred. This question cannot be answered apart from a careful study of Clause C. The error into which JWs fall here is the tacit assumption that "the Word was God" would necessarily mean "the Word was the Father." Orthodox Christianity denies this interpretation, believing John to mean that the Word was with God (the Father) and that the Word was God by nature (the Son). A fully expanded translation-paraphrase of John 1:1 that brings out the shift as understood by trinitarian interpreters might read as follows:

In the beginning the Word was existing;
and the Word was existing in relationship with the person
    commonly known as God, that is, the Father;
and the Word was Himself essentially God.

There is nothing contradictory about saying that the Word was with God and was God as long as "God" is used in two distinct senses in the sentence. Indeed, the JWs themselves believe that "God" is used in two different senses in John 1:1; where they go wrong is in denying that the second person is just as much God by nature as the first person. The question, then, becomes which interpretation is warranted by John's wording.

It is thus wrongheaded to criticize the trinitarian interpretation of John 1:1 as if it assumed that "God" has exactly the same significance in Clause B as in Clause C. One JW publication argued that if "God" is understood to mean the Trinity, then John 1:1 would mean that the Word was with the Trinity and was the Trinity; or if "God" is taken to refer to the Father, then the Word was with the Father and was the Father![16] Such reasoning is extremely superficial and ignores what trinitarian interpreters actually say the text means.

It might be asked on what basis the trinitarian would interpret "God" in Clause B to mean "God the Father" and "God" in Clause C to mean God and yet refer not to the Father but to the Son. The answer to this question must await a careful study of Clause C, which we will begin in the next chapter.

# 2

## The Case of the Missing Article

The usual translation of John 1:1c "and the Word was God" can be misunderstood, as it commonly is by the JWs, to imply that the Word was the same person as the person with whom he existed in the beginning, which would of course be nonsense. For this reason, many biblical translators and commentators favor translating Clause C "and the Word was God by nature" or "essential Deity" or some equivalent rendering, to make it clear that John is making the Word fully God yet personally distinct from the person called "God" in Clause B. If we used definite articles the way John did, the translation, "In the beginning was the Word, and the Word was with the God, and the Word was God," might be best; but to translate "with the God," though literal in its word-for-word correspondence, is awkward English. The translation, "In the beginning was the Word, and the Word was with the Deity, and the Word was Deity," is perhaps as nearly literal a translation as possible that brings out the distinction that John was attempting to make. The one chief defect of this translation is that we do not usually render *theos* in the New Testament as "Deity," so that it sounds somewhat strange to our ears; but it is still perhaps the closest we can come without paraphrasing.

The JWs wish to interpret John 1:1 to mean that the Word was a divine being of some sort, but of a lesser and inferior

27

kind as compared to the one called God in Clause B. To back up this interpretation, they have over the years appealed to numerous translations, commentaries, articles, grammatical textbooks, and other scholarly sources which they feel lend credence to their interpretation. Sorting through what these various sources have said, and learning through careful study what they actually meant, will show that in almost every instance the JWs have misunderstood the sources they quote. Furthermore, a careful study of the grammatical principles at issue will show that the trinitarian interpretation rests securely on the entire body of relevant evidence, and that there is no reasonable possibility of the JW interpretation being correct.

## Definition of Terms

Unfortunately, there are a great deal of technical and semi-technical terms used in discussing the nuances of the Greek language found in John 1:1 and other texts used for comparison purposes. It will be necessary to discuss how these terms are used before proceeding. A key point to observe in this connection is that scholars tend to use terms in somewhat different ways, and misunderstanding will abound if these subtle differences are not identified and kept in mind. It is also extremely important to note that not all dictionary definitions of all these terms will necessarily apply or include the nuances of some of these terms as used by biblical scholars (although such standard dictionaries as *Webster's* can be used to verify most of the following definitions).

We may first discuss the terms *grammar* (and *grammatical*) and *syntax* (and *syntactical*). *Grammar* is a general term used for the study of words and their functions and interrelationships in sentences. *Syntax* refers to the study of word order in sentences—how the order in which words appear in a sentence affects the meaning of the sentence (for example, in English compare "You are here" with "Are you here?" and "Here you are!"). Sometimes scholars treat syntax as a branch of grammar; at other times grammar and syntax are treated as two divisions of the study of a language (with grammar focusing on the spelling, form, and function of individual words treated in isolation).

The word *literal* is generally used to mean that which corresponds as closely as possible with the original wording, as opposed to a *paraphrase* (in which the original wording is abandoned in favor of an alternate wording which is felt to communicate the original *meaning* clearer in English than a literal translation would). There are relative degrees of literalness and paraphrasing. For example, the opening words of John 3:16 in the King James Version (KJV), "For God so loved the world . . ." may be called a "literal" translation, insofar as it represents as accurate a rendering of the original in English as the differences between the two languages permit. However, this "literal" translation completely changes the word order, as it must to be intelligible English. We might say that a more "literal" rendering would be, "so for loved God the world." However, that would not make the KJV rendering any less accurate. An example of a paraphrase of these words might be, "For God the Father loved the human race so much. . . ." Another example is the fact, already pointed out at the beginning of this chapter, that translating John 1:1b "and the Word was with *the* God" is not necessarily the best translation, even though it is the most "literal," that is, closest to a word-for-word translation, because English idiom requires us to drop the definite article in this context.

Sometimes "literal" is contrasted not with "paraphrased" or the like, but with "figurative." *Figurative* language is the use of words to represent, picture, or suggest concepts or images relating to things other than signified by the usual meaning of the words. It involves using what are usually called "figures of speech," which can be classified into various subcategories of figurative language (metaphor, simile, allegory, irony, and so forth). "Jack is a nut" is a sentence using a common metaphor in which the word *nut* is used to represent someone who is crazy, unbalanced, obsessed (thus, "Jack is a football nut"), or similarly odd. It would be a mistake to ask "what Jack and [literal] nuts have in common," because the metaphorical use of the word *nut* has really nothing to do with any properties about nuts that are also inherent in obsessed or mentally unbalanced persons!

Then there are a number of terms used to state whether or not a noun has a definite article ("the") in front of it. The words *anarthrous* and *nonarticular* both mean that the word does not have the definite article, while the words *arthrous* and *articular* both mean that the noun does have the article in front of it. Of these, anarthrous and articular seem to be most common, but our purpose here is to understand the terms, not evaluate them as to how standard they are. Because the word for "God" *(theos)* in John 1:1c does not have a definite article in front of it, it is said to be anarthrous; thus, this term will appear quite a bit in discussions of John 1:1.

The terms *definite* and *indefinite* would seem straightforward enough, but they have turned out to be used in slightly different senses depending on the scholarly source using them. It is natural to understand *definite* to mean "articular" and *indefinite* to mean "anarthrous," and so these terms are occasionally used, but usually not. Most often, *definite* is used of a noun that refers to a specific, identifiable person or thing. For example, in the sentence, "Joe is going to the hospital," *hospital* is articular, but not necessarily definite, because in American English idiom "the hospital" could be any hospital. However, if Joe is a doctor who works at a certain hospital, then in that context "the hospital" probably would be definite. In other words, the same noun in the same exact sentence might be definite in one context and not definite in another context. In the sentence "Mary is going home," *home* is anarthrous, yet definite, because there is a specific home in view (that is, Mary's). Furthermore, in both of these sentences, the subject is anarthrous yet quite definite ("Joe," "Mary"). This is because proper names in English do not normally require the definite article to be definite.

The word *indefinite* is usually used to mean simply any noun that is not definite, that is, which does not refer to a specific, identifiable person or thing. However, sometimes the word is used specifically to refer to a noun that in English has an indefinite article *(a, an)* in front of it. In the sentence, "An old man is king," both nouns *man* and *king* are indefinite in the usual sense, but only "man" is indefinite in the second, more narrow, sense.

With the above definitions of *definite* and *indefinite* in view, a key observation may be made. A noun's being definite or indefinite affects whether or not it has reference to a specific person or thing, but not the basic meaning of the word. In "Joe is going to the hospital," the word *hospital* has the same meaning whether it is definite or indefinite; in either case it refers to an institution which gives medical or surgical care to the sick or injured. However, if it is definite, it should be possible from some preceding context to determine which hospital.

To further complicate matters, the same language can use the definite article in different ways, depending on the period or geographical location of the speaker. In the USA we would say, "Mary is in the hospital," with "the hospital" normally being used generically, with no specific hospital indicated. In Britain, however, the same sentence would usually be worded, "Mary is in hospital," yet with absolutely no change in meaning. Although in the American idiom *hospital* is arthrous while in British idiom it is anarthrous, in both cases "hospital" is indefinite. Similar variations in the use of the definite article can be detected in Greek, depending on the period or even the geographical area of the writer.

Another two words that require definition are *distributed* and *undistributed*. A distributed term is one which represents every member of the class of persons or things named by that term, while an undistributed term does not. In the sentence "Mary is a mother," the term *Mary* is distributed, while *mother* is undistributed (not every mother is Mary, but the one person meant by the name Mary is a mother). In the sentence "All mothers are women," *mothers* is distributed, while *women* is not (not all women are mothers). Note that the *meaning* of a word like *mother* does not change depending on whether it is distributed or not; only its logical function in the sentence changes.

Particularly important and tricky words are *qualitative* and *adjectival*. Much of the debate over the meaning of John 1:1c in recent years has reduced to a debate about the meaning especially of the term *qualitative* as used by certain biblical scholars. As used by grammarians, a noun is said to be "qualitative" if its function in the sentence is primarily to indicate the essential qualities, characteristics, nature, or attributes of something. The term *adjectival* is used more or less synonymously. "Adjectival" simply means functioning as an adjective; and an adjective is a word that describes something. In the sentence "George was a man," the word *man* is, of course, indefinite; it may also be qualitative or adjectival, in the sense that it functions primarily to describe the person identified by the noun *George*. Again, however, this does not change the meaning of the word; in the sentences "George was a man" and "The man you saw was George," the word *man* refers to the same kind of being in both cases. In other words, a noun's being qualitative or adjectival (as well as definite or indefinite) alters its function in the sentence and its specific significance, but not its basic meaning.

It is also important to distinguish between *qualitative* and *figurative* uses of a noun. A noun is used qualitatively if it functions to identify one or more essential characteristics of something. It is used figuratively if it functions in something other than its normal or customary ("literal") usage. "Herod is a man" is qualitative; "Herod is a fox" is figurative. While a noun may be used indefinitely and qualitatively, or indefinitely and figuratively, the concepts of qualitative and figurative should not be confused.

The word *generic* somewhat overlaps in meaning with *qualitative*, but is somewhat distinct. A word is used "generically" when it is used to refer to any or every thing that goes by that name. In the sentence "Man is a rational animal," the word *man* is used generically, because it stands for all those who may be called "man" (including men and women).

A *predicate noun* is a noun which functions as the predicate or subject complement in a sentence. The word *man* is a predicate noun in each of the following sentences: "George was a man"; "George was the man"; "George is a tall man"; "My friend George was at one time an important man in the town." In John 1:1c, "and the Word was God," *God (theos)* is a predicate noun. The term *predicate nominative* is also used frequently for a predicate noun, because the noun is in the nominative case (see discussion of "nominative" in chapter 1).

The terms *nature, essence* (and *essential*), *character* (and *characteristic*), and *being* are roughly synonymous terms as used in this context. They are all used by scholars to refer to that collection of basic properties or attributes that makes a thing what it is, that which marks out what kind of thing it is, and sets it apart from other things. The term *nature* has the specific idea of that which comes intrinsically and normally from within the thing named. (The JWs are in error when they argue that, because etymologically the word *nature* stems from a word meaning "born," it is improper to speak of God as having a "nature."[1] They fail to appreciate the fact that a word can have a meaning which goes beyond its original formation or etymological roots.) A thing's "essence" is that without which it would not be what it is: for example, a mind is essential to a human being; fingers, though normally part of every human being, are not essential to humanness. The "character" of a thing is its basic type, kind, or sort; a "characteristic" is one aspect of a thing's character, an identifying mark. Although the word *character* certainly can be used to refer to a person's moral disposition, this is not the usual meaning in the context of a grammatical analysis. *Being* is a word sometimes used synonymously with "essence," and refers to that which is, the thing itself as it exists independently of other things.

Finally, something should be said about the various words for deity. The word *God* in English Judeo-Christian usage refers generally to the God called Yahweh ("Jehovah") in the Old Testament—biblically, the true God, the only real God. The word *god* is used occasionally as a translation of the Hebrew *el* or Greek *theos* without regard for whether it refers to the true God or not; most often as a term for anything other than the true God regarded by men as worthy of worship (and thus for false gods); and by henotheists (those who believe that there are many gods, only one of which deserves worship) as a term used for beings considered to be genuinely worthy of some sort of religious honor, even though viewed as inferior to the real God. The English distinction between *God* and *god* is not found in all languages. German, for example, always capitalizes "Gott," whether or not it refers to the true God, because in German all nouns must be capitalized.

The word *godlike* means something that is not actually a god, but is like a god, or even like God in certain respects, probably including the notion of a being possessing great power.

The word *divine* indicates either that something belongs to God (or a god) or is characteristic of God (or a god), depending on who is using the term and in what context. Biblical scholars often use the term to mean that which is characteristic of God, or even to mean that which possesses the nature of God. The word *deity* generally refers either to the essence of God or, in a polytheistic context, to anything regarded as a god. The word *Deity* refers specifically to the single God of monotheism, to the being of God.

On the difference between *divine* and *deity*, Ed. L. Miller writes:

> It would appear that for most there is a difference in affirming of *x* that it is "divine" and that it is "deity." It is the difference between some sort of participation in or likeness to deity and deity itself. Clearly, "divine" is weaker and more ambiguous a term than "deity" and "God."[2]

In evangelical circles this is certainly true, and for this reason evangelicals tend to dismiss the rendering "the Word was divine" (see Goodspeed, Moffatt) as somehow a denial of the deity of Christ. However, this is not necessarily the case (although sometimes it is). For many theologians and scholars the word *divine* is simply an adjectival form of "divinity," the old term for "deity," so that in their terminology "the Word was divine" would mean "the Word was deity" or the equivalent. For example, Bruce Vawter commented on John 1:1, "The Word is divine, but he is not all of divinity, for he has already been distinguished from another divine Person."[3] Here *divine* is simply an adjectival form of *divinity*, which is equivalent to *deity* in Vawter's terminology, as can be seen from the fact that elsewhere Vawter refers to "the three divine Persons" of the Trinity.[4] Harner is quite right, then, when he comments:

> Undoubtedly Vawter means that the Word is "divine" in the same sense that *ho theos* is divine. But the English language is not as versatile at this point as Greek, and we can avoid misunderstanding the English phrase only if we are aware of the particular force of the Greek expression that it represents.[5]

## The Absence of the Article

In John 1:1c, there are two nouns in the nominative case (that is, the case in which nouns are used as the subject), *theos* and *logos*. These two nouns are connected by a form of the verb "to be" (called by grammarians a "linking verb" or "copula"), in this case the verb *ēn* ("was"). If this were all we knew, it would be difficult to determine which noun was the subject and which was the predicate (or, as it is sometimes called, the subject complement). In other words, we might not know whether John's point was that "God was Word" or "Word was God." The word order in Greek places the word *theos* first, but this does not necessarily mean that *theos* is the subject, since in Greek the subject often appears in the middle or at the end of the sentence (unlike English, in which the subject usually appears toward the beginning of the sentence or clause).

However, there is one other piece of information. The definite article *ho* appears in front of *logos* but not in front of *theos*. Thus, the clause reads, *theos ēn ho logos*. The use of the article in front of *logos* but not in front of *theos*—whatever else this may mean—indicates, according to biblical grammarians, that *logos* is the subject of the clause. Thus, we should translate "The Word was God" not "God was the Word" when rendering the clause into English, even though the latter translation follows the Greek word order exactly, since such a translation implies, in English, that "God" is the subject of the clause, whereas in fact "Word" is the subject.

This distinction has been explained, for example, by A. T. Robertson:

> The subject is made plain by the article *(ho logos)* and the predicate without it *(theos)* just as in John 4:24 *pneuma ho theos* can only mean "God is spirit," not "spirit is God." So in I John 4:16 *ho theos agapē estin* can only mean "God is love," not "love is God" as a so-called Christian scientist [i.e., follower of Mary Baker Eddy] would confusedly say. For the article with the predicate see Robertson, *Grammar*, pp. 767f. So in John 1:14 *ho Logos sarx egeneto*, "the Word became flesh," not "the flesh became Word."[6]

C. H. Dodd, in commenting on John 1:1, makes the same point:

> On the other hand[7] it may be argued that the absence of the article is a purely grammatical phenomenon. The general rule is that in a sentence containing the verb "to be" as a copula the subject has the article and a predicate noun is anarthrous, even though it be definite. Hence, if *theos* was to be used predicatively it would be anarthrous, without any necessary change of meaning from the *ho theos* of the preceding clause.

Purely grammatical considerations therefore do not close the question.[8]

Examples could easily be multiplied but need not. There is absolutely no dispute among biblical scholars and Greek grammarians that in John 1:1 *logos* is the subject and *theos* the predicate, and that this is indicated by the presence of the article with *logos* and its absence with *theos*. So much at least may be regarded as incontrovertible fact (not even disputed by the Witnesses). The question is whether there is any further significance to the omission of the article before *theos*.

There is, besides the lack of the article before *theos*, another bit of information that is generally regarded as significant for correctly interpreting the meaning of *theos*—namely, the order of the words in the clause. Now, in some respects the order of words is not nearly so significant in Greek as in English. For example, as has already been noted, English tends to keep the subject toward the beginning of the main clause, whereas Greek can have the subject in the middle or at the end of the sentence or clause. However, this comparative lack of importance of word order or syntax should not be exaggerated into the completely erroneous claim that word order is irrelevant or insignificant in Greek. Such is not the case. Several volumes on the subject of Greek syntax have been written in this century, all of them testifying to the many ways in which word order can affect the precise meaning of Greek sentences.[9] Therefore, the possibility that the word order used in John 1:1c might reflect a particular shade of meaning ought at least to be considered.

What most biblical scholars who have discussed John 1:1 in detail have found particularly significant about the word order of Clause C is the fact that the anarthrous predicate nominative *theos* precedes the linking verb *ēn* ("was"). In other words, it has generally been agreed that John's writing *theos ēn ho logos* instead of *ho logos ēn theos* is somehow significant. The placement of *theos* before the verb instead of after it is thought to indicate a different nuance of some sort.

We have, then, two facts about the precise wording of
John 1:1 which biblical scholars believe to be somehow significant for the exact meaning of the sentence: 1) The word
*theos* is anarthrous, while *logos* is arthrous; and 2) the word
*theos* stands before the linking verb, not after. The first fact,
all agree, indicates that *logos* is the subject and *theos* the predicate; the question is whether there is any other significance
to this fact. The second fact is generally regarded as also
somehow significant, especially when taken together with
the first fact.

In what follows we shall seek to examine the evidence
carefully to see what the reason is for the particular wording
which John used. We shall examine some of the theories
scholars have put forth to explain the significance of the
word order and the absence of the article before *theos*. What
we shall learn will prove beyond any reasonable doubt that
the JWs' interpretation of John 1:1 is completely untenable.

# 3

# Definite or Indefinite?

A great deal of confusion over John 1:1 swirls about the grammatical terminology used, as has already been noted. This is particularly true with respect to the terms *definite*, *indefinite*, and *qualitative*. It has often been assumed—by both JWs and Christians—that if and only if *theos* in John 1:1 is definite, then "the Word was God" is correct, while if *theos* is admitted to be either qualitative or indefinite in any sense, then the JWs are vindicated and "the Word was a god" is justified. This assumption is unwarranted.

The word *definite*, as has already been explained, is used of a noun that refers to a specific, identifiable person or thing, whether or not the noun has a definite article in front of it (either in English or in the other language), while *indefinite* refers to any noun that is not "definite." The confusion comes in thinking that it is always legitimate to translate an indefinite noun with an indefinite article *a* or *an* in English. This is certainly not the case. For example, we would not normally translate abstract nouns with an indefinite article even when the usage is indefinite. Titles may or may not take an indefinite article when they are indefinite. We should not, therefore, equate "indefinite" nouns in Greek with indefinite translations in English.

So, for example, in the sentence ". . . God is love" (1 John 4:8), we would never translate the indefinite abstract noun *love* as "a love." In our earlier example sentence "An old man is king," we would not normally render the indefinite title "king" as "a king"; but the sentence "George is king" could be modified to read, "George is a king." Most important to notice here is that the meaning of "king" does not really change; only its significance in the context of the sentence varies slightly.

To understand what it would mean to assert that in John 1:1c *theos* is definite, it is helpful to reconsider the significance of *ton theon* in the preceding clause. We noted in our earlier discussion of that clause that the orthodox interpretation of "the Word was with God" was that "the Word was existing in relationship with the person commonly known as God, that is, the Father" (chapter 1), but did not offer a thorough defense of that interpretation. The key here is the articular *ton theon*. One of the most basic uses of the definite article in Greek (and in English as well), beyond purely grammatical functions, is to identify the subject of the noun as one already known to the listeners or readers.

> The function of the article is to point out (it was in origin a demonstrative), to determine, to set apart from others, to identify as *this* or *these* and not simply "such." We can therefore always be sure that the use of the article shows the thing spoken of to have been in the author's mind (or in that of those whose speech-habits established current usage) determinate and familiar. . . .[1]

The text before us is the opening line of the Gospel of John and therefore the first use in that book of *theos*. In this context the use of the definite article in the expression *pros ton theon* clearly serves to identify as *theon* ("God") the person commonly known to John's readers (who accepted the God of the Old Testament as the true God) as such—specifically, the person whom Jesus called "the Father," and whom the apostles later were to call "God the Father." That is, *ton theon* in John 1:1b refers specifically to God the Father. This conclusion is shown to be correct by the references later in the

"Prologue" to John's Gospel to the Father as the One with whom the Word existed (John 1:14, 18).

The significance of *theon* being definite in Clause B, then, is to identify the One spoken of there as a specific person—God the Father. If, then, *theos* in Clause C were to be "definite" in the same way that *theon* is in Clause B, it would then be saying that the Word was God the Father. Such a statement would contradict Clause B and imply some sort of modalistic view of God, which of course trinitarians oppose (though JWs often misconstrue the doctrine of the Trinity as teaching modalism[2]).

This conclusion—that *theos* in Clause C could not be definite without contradicting Clause B and implying heresy—should not be misunderstood to be a denial that Jesus is God. First of all, it must be remembered that what is indefinite in Greek need not—and sometimes *must* not—be translated with an indefinite article in English. The reason why it would be incorrect to translate *theos* "a god" shall be made clear as we progress; the fact is that such a rendering is not necessitated by *theos* being indefinite. Second, the point that is being made here is that for *theos* to be definite *in this context*—after just using the definite *ton theon* to refer specifically to the person of the Father—would be modalistic. This does not mean that *theos* cannot ever be definite when applied to Christ, nor does it mean that Christ cannot be called *theos* with the definite article *ho*. Christ is, in fact, called "God" with the definite article in several other texts (John 20:28; Titus 2:13; 2 Peter 1:1; 1 John 5:20).[3] It is true, however, that none of these passages calls Christ simply *ho theos* without qualification, evidently because this expression was so firmly associated with the person of the Father. Thus he is called "my God," "our God and Savior," "our great God and Savior," and "the true God and eternal life"—all using the definite article, all indisputably identifying Christ as the Almighty God of the Old Testament, but all avoiding identifying him as the person of the Father.

Therefore, those who have argued that in John 1:1 *theos* is definite were in error.[4] However, in some cases the point they were trying to make was a valid one. A careful study of the arguments of those who have said that *theos* is definite will reveal that often what they meant was that *theos* should be translated "God" rather than "a god." In other words, they were talking about how the word should be *translated*, not about whether it was actually definite or indefinite in the Greek text. Their mistake was in attributing to the Greek word *theos* the apparent definiteness of the English word "God" generally used to translate *theos*.

To say then that in John 1:1c *theos* is indefinite is to say nothing more than that the Word is not being identified as the specific person of the Father. As surprising as it may seem, arguing that *theos* is definite in this context actually is inconsistent with the trinitarian distinction between the Father and the Son.

What though does it mean to say that *theos* is qualitative? It needs to be clarified immediately that "qualitative" is not a third category of noun analysis; that is, nouns do not fall neatly into three baskets marked DEFINITE, INDEFINITE, and QUALITATIVE. Rather, *qualitative* is a term that can apply to both definite and indefinite nouns. It refers to a noun, whether definite or indefinite (though the latter is more common), which in context expresses "the nature or character of the subject."[5] As has already been explained in chapter 2, the qualitative use of a noun does not alter its basic meaning, but simply gives it a particular nuance which emphasizes the subject's characteristics or qualities as such. For instance, the word "king" in the sentences "George was a king" and "The king was George" means the same thing exactly in both instances, but in the second sentence refers to a specific king while in the first it emphasizes George's nature or function.

To say that in John 1:1c *theos* is "qualitative," then, does not imply that *theos* means anything less than it means in 1:1b. It is simply another way of saying that the Word is called God with reference to his nature, essence, or being, and does not identify the Word as a specific person. This can be seen by examining other instances of the qualitative use of the noun, as we shall demonstrate shortly. At this point, however, it is necessary to examine more closely the misuse of the term "qualitative" by the JWs in the service of their "a god" rendering, and their use of alleged "parallels" in support.

## Indefinite Parallels to John 1:1

In recent years a list of parallels to John 1:1 has been presented by the JWs in a chart published in the 1984 Reference Edition of the NWT and drawn from Nelson Herle's manuscript on the Trinity.[6] This chart lists eleven verses containing anarthrous predicate nouns preceding the verb, each of which in most translations is normally rendered with an indefinite article. The example most often cited from this list is John 6:70, where Jesus says to his disciples (regarding Judas Iscariot), ". . . one of you is a devil" (or, a slanderer; the word is *diabolos*). Here the predicate noun *diabolos* precedes the verb *estin* ("is").

Such texts are indeed examples of the fact that anarthrous predicate nominatives preceding the verb *can*, in some cases, be indefinite, and can even be rendered with the indefinite article *a* or *an*. This does not disturb the interpretation of John 1:1 presented here, however, because our position is that *theos* in John 1:1 is "indefinite" in the sense of being used generically. Furthermore, not all indefinite nouns should be rendered with *a* or *an*, as has already been explained.

A careful look at the nouns in the New Testament which are anarthrous and precede the verb and should be translated with the indefinite article reveals that *the nouns never change their basic meaning as a result of being used or even translated indefinitely.* This point shall be thoroughly documented later in this chapter.

The most thorough treatment of indefinite anarthrous predicates as compared to John 1:1 by a JW appears to be by Nelson Herle. Herle comments on the meaning of five such texts (Mark 11:32; John 6:70; 8:44; 10:2; 12:6), and then offers the following explanation of the "qualitative" use of a noun:

> Use of this type of expression in our everyday speech is common. "He is a brain" = 'he is intelligent'; "he is a Caruso" = 'he is a great singer': "she is an angel" = 'she is sweet, compassionate'; "he is a Spartan" = 'he is brave, highly disciplined, hardy'. In English, the same word order is used in both an indefinite and qualitative significance; however, emphasis or word stress shows the difference. In Greek, this is accomplished by word order; the verb before or after the noun. . . .
>
> With this it is clear what is meant by the phrase, "the Word was a god"; the Word was, godlike, holy, righteous, divine and virtuous. The Word was not "the God"; not "God"; not "*a* god", that is 'one of the gods'; the Word was, "a *god*."[7]

Herle has made a number of mistakes here, the most basic of which is that he has confused the concepts of figurative and qualitative (*see* the discussion of these terms above in chapter 2). The anarthrous predicate noun preceding the verb can be used figuratively (for example, "a sweet odor," 2 Cor. 2:15 NWT), but this is incidental to the grammar or syntax, as has already been explained. Of the five "parallels" Herle discusses, at least three must be taken in the usual, literal sense ("prophet," Mark 11:32; "manslayer" and "liar," John 8:44; "thief," John 12:6). Indeed, the meaning of these words in their contexts is quite straightforward and much simpler than Herle's explanations would suggest. For example, in John 12:6 we read that Judas "was a thief" (NWT); Herle's interpretation is as follows:

> He was not merely *a* thief, one who stole. But he was a *thief,* he want[ed] to steal; his nature was to steal; stealing was in his heart. He was a *thief!*[8]

This rather elaborate interpretation has no basis in the qualitative use of a noun as understood by grammarians, nor is there any reason to interpret generally anarthrous predicate nouns preceding the verb in this manner, as a study of such passages will make clear.

## Analysis of Grammatical Parallels

At this point, we are ready for a comprehensive look at anarthrous predicate nouns preceding the verb. In the following analysis various categories of usage have been identified. Some of these may rightly be regarded as overlapping. Furthermore, some of the specific texts may be variously categorized, depending on the precise interpretation of the text. It is not always easy to tell whether a noun is definite or indefinite. Still, that these various kinds of usages can be found should not be doubted. Finally, these lists are as complete as I have been able to make them, although no claim is made to being exhaustive.[9]

*Definite-Qualitative.* These are nouns which appear from the context to be referring to one definite or specific individual person or thing (whether or not it is the only one ever identified by that noun). In most of these contexts a "qualitative" aspect is evident, though not necessarily prominent.

| | |
|---|---|
| God | Phil. 2:13; Heb. 11:16 |
| Lord of the sabbath | Matt. 12:8; Mark 2:28; Luke 6:5 |
| Lord = unique Lord | Rev. 17:14 |
| Lord = Jehovah (NWT) | 1 Cor. 4:4 |
| King (of Israel/the Jews) | Matt. 27:42; John 1:49; 19:21 |
| Son of man[10] | John 5:27 |
| Leader | Matt. 23:10 |
| bridegroom | John 3:29 |
| high priest | John 11:49, 51 |
| Abraham | John 8:39 |

| light | John 9:5 |
| shepherd | John 10:2 |
| mediator | Heb. 9:15 |
| Sinai | Gal. 4:25 |
| propitiatory sacrifice | 1 John 2:2 |
| footstool | Matt. 5:35 |
| city | Matt. 5:35 |

These nouns are "definite" in that they have specific reference to one person or thing, even though in most cases there is also a qualitative aspect to the noun. Some of them in English must even be translated with a definite article, and none would normally be translated with an indefinite article (though note Hebrews 9:15 and 1 John 2:2 in the NWT).

It is noteworthy that in two instances an anarthrous predicate *theos* preceding the verb must be considered definite and translated "God." In Philippians 2:13 the usual translation, "God is the one working in you," may not be exactly right, because *ho energōn* ("the one working"), with the article, is apparently the subject, and *theos*, without the article, is evidently the predicate. If this is so, then a more accurate rendering in English might be "The one who is working in you is God." This interpretation also fits the context well; after urging the Philippians to work out their salvation (2:12), Paul reminds them that the one who will actually effect this working out is none other than God. In the other text, Hebrews 11:16, a literal translation would be "God is not ashamed of them, to be called upon by them as God." The second "God" is anarthrous, and is clearly qualitative. In neither Philippians 2:13 nor Hebrews 11:16 can the word *theos* be translated anything other than "God."

Another text worth noting, though not listed above, is Romans 8:33b, usually translated, "God is the one who justifies." The Greek reads *theos ho dikaiōn*, with no linking verb expressed (which is why it is not listed above, because there is no verb for the predicate noun to precede). However, in a case similar to Philippians 2:13, it would probably be more accurate to translate "the one who justifies is God."

As we have already explained, *theos* in John 1:1 should not be interpreted strictly speaking as "definite," in the sense that *ton theon* is definite in the second clause of the verse. However, the examples of Philippians 2:13 and Hebrews 11:16 demonstrate that a qualitative use of the anarthrous *theos* does not shift its meaning from "God" to "a god."

*Qualitative-Indefinite.* These are nouns which are clearly being used generically, with no sense of definiteness, and which are regularly translated in English with the indefinite article.

| | |
|---|---|
| a God | Mark 12:27; Luke 20:38 |
| an apparition | Matt. 14:26; Mark 6:49 |
| a prophet | Mark 11:32; John 4:19; 9:17 |
| a man | Luke 5:8; John 10:33; Acts 10:26; James 5:17 |
| a woman | John 4:9 |
| a slanderer | John 6:70 |
| a manslayer/murderer | John 8:44; Acts 28:4 |
| a liar | John 8:44; 1 John 2:4 |
| a beggar | John 9:8 |
| a sinner | John 9:24, 25 |
| a thief | John 10:1; 12:6 |
| a hired man | John 10:13 |
| a relative | John 18:26 |
| a king | John 18:37 [2 times] |
| a vessel | Acts 9:15 |
| a sweet odor | 2 Cor. 2:15 |

a babe                          Gal. 4:1; Heb. 5:13

a debtor                        Gal. 5:3 (NWT literally reads
                                "under obligation")

None of these words takes on a lesser or weakened meaning because of being used "qualitatively" or "indefinitely."
The men are men, the woman is a woman, the sinner is a
sinner, the king is a king, in the usual, fullest sense of the
words. As mentioned before, some of these words are, of
course, used figuratively (such as *babe* and *sweet odor*), but
this is quite another matter, and has nothing whatever to do
with their being indefinite or qualitative. (Many definite
nouns are also figurative, for instance, John 4:14, "the
water"; 6:41, "the bread"; 8:12, "the light"; 10:7, "the door";
and so forth.) The JWs generally do not argue that the Word
is called "a god" only in a figurative sense. Rather, they argue
for a weakened or limited literal use of the word *theos* in John
1:1, with the meaning of a powerful entity of some sort. They
argue that *theos* in 1:1c means a god of a lesser deity than *ton
theon*, "God," in 1:1b. Such a shift in meaning in *theos* is
inconsistent with the indefinite use of Greek nouns, as the
above list demonstrates.

Particularly startling are Mark 12:27 and Luke 20:38, parallel passages in which Jesus calls the true God "a God." Luke
20:37–38 reads as follows in the NWT:

But that the dead are raised up even Moses disclosed, in the
account about the thornbush, when he calls Jehovah 'the God
of Abraham and God of Isaac and God of Jacob. He is a God,
not of the dead, but of the living, for they are all living to
him.'

Jehovah, then, is "a God," according to the JWs' own
translation! If this were the "qualitative" or "indefinite" sense
to which the JWs attributed *theos* in John 1:1, there would be
no problem. In that case, we would understand the expression "a God" as we do in Luke 20:38 and Mark 12:27, not as

implying one God in contrast to another God, or a deity of a lesser nature in comparison to another deity, but simply as speaking of the only true God from the standpoint of his nature—what kind of "a God" he is. An interesting point to note is that in the parallel text in Matthew (22:32) some critical Greek texts (including the Westcott-Hort, upon which the NWT is based) have the definite article in front of *theos*. Thus, the NWT reads in Matthew 22:32, "He is *the* God, not of the dead . . ." (italics mine), without, of course, implying any difference in the essential meaning of "God" between the verse in Matthew and the other two gospels.

It needs to be stated as explicitly as possible that the problem with the "a god" rendering of John 1:1 is not merely the word *a*, or even the lower-case spelling, although in English that is highly misleading. It is, most fundamentally, how that rendering is interpreted in its context. (That the failure to capitalize "god" is significant only because of English idiom can be illustrated by comparing it to German. In German, the NWT rendering of John 1:1c would literally be "und das Wort war ein Gott"—capitalizing "Gott," because in German, as has already been mentioned, all nouns must be capitalized.) In English, rendering "a god" in John 1:1 can only be interpreted as making the Word a different—and lesser—deity than the God with whom he was in the beginning.

Putting John 1:1 into the category of qualitative-indefinite nouns, therefore, would not be wrong, as long as "a God" were interpreted in the same way as in Mark 12:27 and Luke 20:38. However, because in English "a God," but especially "a god," would in the context of John 1:1 (unlike that of Mark 12:27 and Luke 20:38) suggest to most readers a second (and probably inferior) deity, and since this idea is not conveyed by the anarthrous predicate *theos*, such a rendering is to be rejected.

*Qualitative of Substance or Essence.* These nouns are used to identify the substance, essence, or nature of something (whether literally or with figurative language). This category could be regarded as a subset of the indefinite-qualitative category, with the modification that in English we do not normally use the indefinite article with these words. It is noteworthy that all of them appear in John's writings.

flesh   John 1:14; 3:6

spirit   John 3:6; 6:63 (cf. 4:24)

life      John 6:63; 12:50

wine   John 2:9

truth   John 17:17

light    1 John 1:5

love    1 John 4:8

It is arguable that *theos* in John 1:1 belongs squarely in this category. Since this category could be regarded as a subset of the indefinite-qualitative category, there would be no conflict with putting John 1:1 in this category as well as that one. The difference would be that in English we would not translate "a God" if the noun were regarded as expressive of nature or essence, as with the examples listed above. As it turns out, most biblical scholars and commentators do place John 1:1 into this category, as shall be shown later in this study.

*Adjectival-Qualitative.* These words are adjectives, not nouns, in form, and it is a matter of preference whether they are translated as substantives in these contexts. For example, *Galilaios ei* can be translated "you are a Galilean" or "you are Galilean."

| | |
|---|---|
| Galilean | Mark 14:70; Luke 22:59; 23:6 |
| Samaritan | John 8:48 |
| Jew | John 4:9; 18:35 |
| Hebrews, Israelites | 2 Cor. 11:22 |
| Pharisee | Acts 23:6 |

| | |
|---|---|
| Greek | Acts 16:3 |
| Roman(s) | Acts 16:21, 37; 22:27, 29; 23:27 |
| good | John 7:12 (or, as in NWT, "a good man") |

Since there is no question that John 1:1 does not fit this usage of the anarthrous predicate, this category of usage may be regarded as irrelevant to John 1:1.

*Qualitative of Relationship.* These nouns are used to identify a certain personal relationship. They are neither specifically definite or indefinite as a rule, although in a few cases the noun can be construed as either definite or indefinite.

| | |
|---|---|
| YOUR God | John 8:54 (some manuscripts have "your God") |
| YOUR Father | John 8:42 |
| God's (My) Son | Matt. 4:3, 6; 14:33; 27:40, 54; Mark 15:39; Luke 4:3, 9; John 10:36; Acts 13:33; Heb. 1:5; 5:5 (NWT alternates between "a son of God" and "God's Son") |
| David's son | Mark 12:35 |
| Joseph's son | Luke 4:22 (NWT, "a son of Joseph") |
| sons | John 12:36; 1 Thess. 5:5 |
| children | John 1:12; Gal. 4:28 |
| Abraham's children | John 8:39 |
| Abraham's seed | John 8:33, 37 (NWT, "offspring"); 2 Cor. 11:22; Gal. 3:29 |
| brother(s) | Matt. 12:50; 23:8; Mark 3:35; Acts 7:26; 1 Tim. 6:2 |
| sister | Matt. 12:50; Mark 3:35 |
| mother | Matt. 12:50; Mark 3:35 |

| friend(s)        | John 15:14; James 2:23                              |
| disciple(s)      | John 8:31; 9:27, 28; 13:35                          |
| slaves/servants  | John 8:34; Acts 16:17; 2 Cor. 11:23 (NWT, "ministers") |
| minister         | Rom. 13:4 (2 times)                                 |
| public servants  | Rom. 13:6                                           |
| fellow-workers   | 2 Cor. 1:24                                         |

This usage of the anarthrous predicate preceding the verb is extremely common. (The relational use of these terms is not, of course, dependent upon them being used in an anarthrous predicate.) Moreover, the word *God* can be a relational term, as in the expression "your God" (for example, John 8:54 listed above). However, in John 1:1 *theos* is not used with reference to those who honor Christ as God, but rather to denote his deity in the beginning. Therefore, since the word *theos* is not a relational noun in the context of John 1:1, this category is also not directly relevant to John 1:1. If it were, of course, we would also have to translate *theos* as "God," because in the context of biblical faith in which John writes there is only one real *theos* in relation to the universe of created things.

*Qualitative-Nondefinite.*    These nouns are not easily classifiable in any of the above categories.

| throne       | Matt. 5:34                              |
| conclusion   | Matt. 13:39                             |
| angels       | Matt. 13:39                             |
| house        | Mark 11:17; Heb. 3:6                    |
| witness(es)  | Luke 11:48; Acts 3:15; Rom. 1:9         |
| ground       | Acts 7:33                               |
| betrayers    | Acts 7:52                               |

| | |
|---|---|
| sin | Rom. 14:23 |
| foolishness | 1 Cor. 1:18; 2:14; 3:19 |
| power | 1 Cor. 1:18 |
| temple | 1 Cor. 3:16; 6:19; 2 Cor. 6:16; Rev. 21:22 |
| imitators | 1 Cor. 4:16 |
| members | 1 Cor. 6:15 |
| body | 1 Cor. 6:16 |
| root | 1 Tim. 6:10 |
| works | Heb. 1:10 |
| worship | James 1:27 |
| enmity | James 4:4 |

These anarthrous predicates will be placed in the previous categories depending on the precise interpretation of the texts as a whole. The point of this list is to show that although it is not always easy to classify a noun as either definite or indefinite, this does not prevent the reader from grasping the meaning of the word in context. Indeed, the above list confirms the main thesis of this study, which is that nouns do not change their essential meaning when used indefinitely rather than definitely.

Of the several instances of the anarthrous predicate nominative *theos* before the verb, then, not one makes *theos* mean anything less than God (Mark 12:27; Luke 20:38; John 8:54; Phil. 2:13; Heb. 11:16; cf. Rom. 8:33b), unless one counts John 1:1. In the other five clear instances of this use of *theos*, the word can only be translated "God" in English.

# 4

## The Word: "God" or "a God"?

In the preceding chapter we examined the anarthrous predicate nominative in its occurrences before the verb in the New Testament. This analysis demonstrated that the use of this construction does not alter the meaning of the word *theos* or any other word so used. However, the JWs feel that there are other "parallel" passages which prove that the word *theos* can be used to mean "a god" in the sense in which they use that expression. In this chapter we shall examine that claim and try to answer the question of how John 1:1 should be translated.

It is important to realize that examining parallel texts—though useful up to a point—can be overrated and abused. For one thing, partial parallels can only yield partial information about the text being studied. It is too easy to fall into the error of thinking that because two texts share a common feature, other features must also be parallel. One must be careful to consider the differences between the texts being compared, as well as the similarities. This caution is most applicable to a number of alleged parallel texts which the JWs cite as evidence in behalf of their "a god" rendering.

### Acts 28:6

Perhaps the alleged parallel text most often cited by JWs is Acts 28:6, in which Luke reports that the Maltese heathen, astonished at Paul's miraculous escape from harm by a deadly snake, ". . . began saying he was a god" (NWT). The Greek expression here is *elegon auton einai theon*. JWs often cite this verse and point to the fact that the anarthrous *theon* is translated "a god" by virtually all translations as proof that their rendering of *theos* as "a god" in John 1:1 is perfectly legitimate.[1]

This argument overlooks two crucial and easy-to-recognize differences between John 1:1 and Acts 28:6. First of all, *theon* in Acts 28:6 is an anarthrous predicate noun; but it follows the verb *einai* instead of preceding it. As we have already noted, biblical scholars agree that the position of the predicate after the verb instead of before it is significant; how so, we shall see later in the next chapter. Second, Acts 28:6 is reporting the belief of polytheistic pagans, whereas John 1:1 is an inspired affirmation by the apostle John. The Maltese people's conclusion that Paul was *theos* was a superstitious confession that Paul was literally a god, a true god; so that Paul was in that situation, from a biblical perspective— through no fault of his own—a false god wrongly idolized by pagans. On the other hand, John's statement that the Word was *theos* was inspired truth, so that the Word was, from a biblical perspective, really and truly *theos*.

In order to argue that Acts 28:6 legitimizes their rendering of John 1:1, then, JWs must be prepared to argue, first, that the position of the anarthrous predicate noun before the verb instead of after is not at all significant; and second, that the Word was a false god. The first is contrary to the facts, and the second is contrary even to the theology of the JWs.

Although Acts 28:6 is not a legitimate parallel to John 1:1, in the past at least one poor argument against the parallel has been used that ought to be abandoned. In the early 1970s an evangelical apologist asked Dr. J. Johnson, a professor of Greek at California State University, Long Beach, to comment on this alleged parallel. Johnson wrote, "There is no syntactical parallel to Acts 28:6, where there is a statement in indirect discourse, John 1:1 is direct."[2] While it is true that

Acts 28:6 is indirect discourse ("they were saying he was a god"), this difference is of no consequence as to the significance of *theos*, because indirect discourse here affects only the case of the predicate (accusative *theon* instead of nominative *theos*) and the mood of the verb (infinitive *einai* instead of indicative *ēn*).[3] Thus, Christians who are critiquing the JWs' argument based on Acts 28:6 would do well to avoid citing Dr. Johnson's comment.

## Acts 12:22

A second text sometimes cited as proving that *theos* in John 1:1 might be translated "a god" is Acts 12:22, where Luke reports that the people cried out concerning Herod the king, "A god's voice, and not a man's!" (NWT).[4]

This text is even less parallel to John 1:1 than Acts 28:6. The word "god" in Acts 12:22 is anarthrous, but that is where the "parallel" ends. It is in the genitive case (*theou*, used to show possession, "god's"), and is thus not a predicate nominative at all. Also, of course, Herod is being hailed as a god in superstitious unbelief (compare verse 23), and is therefore in this context a false god.

## John 10:33

A third text which might be cited by JWs as proving that *theos* in John 1:1 can legitimately be translated "a god" is John 10:33. In this verse the Jews accuse Jesus of "blasphemy, even because you, although being a man, make yourself a god" (NWT).

In this verse "a god" is in the accusative case (*theon*), as the direct object of the verb *making*. This usage is roughly parallel to that of an anarthrous predicate nominative with a form of the verb "to be."[5] However, as in Acts 28:6, the noun *theon* follows the verb instead of preceding it. Also, once again, the meaning is a false god (assuming the NWT translation to be correct), since the Jews are accusing Jesus of blasphemy by making himself a (false) god.

Of course, it might be possible to translate John 10:33 to say that "you, being a man, are making yourself God." If this translation is correct, Jesus' alleged blasphemy consisted in making himself God. If "making yourself a god" is correct, his alleged blasphemy consisted in considering himself to be a divine being when he was not (in the Jews' opinion). Either way, this verse cannot substantiate the idea that the word *theos* was ever used in the New Testament to mean a genuine or real god, and not a false god, who was other than the God of Israel.

## The Use of THEOS in the New Testament

Jehovah's Witnesses maintain that there are three uses of the term *God* in Scripture: in reference to the true God, Jehovah; in reference to false gods, whether existing creatures or imagined; and a "third use" in reference to creatures which, by virtue of their might and authority over other creatures, are legitimately designated "gods." In this third use of the term, the creatures are neither true gods nor false gods; yet somehow, they are still gods. How they could be neither true gods nor false gods and still be gods is a puzzle. The Witnesses, however, feel that such a conclusion is warranted from the biblical evidence.

The alleged biblical evidence, however, is quite slim. The texts used to document this "third use" are Psalm 82:1, 6 (compare with John 10:34); Psalm 8:5 (compare with Heb. 2:7); and sometimes Exodus 22:8–9, 28. This is very slim evidence indeed, especially when all of the texts can be explained as either referring to God himself or to false gods.

Moreover, it is not to be overlooked that in each case the noun is the Hebrew plural *elohim*, not the Hebrew singular *el* or Greek *theos*. Let us assume for a moment the JWs' view that there are three uses for the word *God* in Scripture. When the Hebrew plural noun *elohim* is used as a plural, or the

Greek plural noun *theoi* (which is always a plural) is used, they clearly cannot be referring to the true God. In such cases, there is no ambiguity as to whether or not the word refers to God himself. Either it refers to God, or to false gods (or, according to the JWs, to creatures which, while not God, are not false gods either, but "gods" in a relative or derivative sense). Only where there is some confusion as to whether or not *elohim* is used as a singular to refer to God or as a plural to refer to creatures considered in some sense "gods" (as there is some confusion concerning Exodus 22:8–9, 28, and Psalm 8:5) is there any ambiguity. However, with the singular nouns for God, and especially with the Greek noun *theos*, there is no such ambiguity.

Since our interest is in the meaning of the singular Greek *theos* in John 1:1, it is legitimate to restrict our attention to the usage of the singular *theos* in the New Testament. Doing so, we find that it is used in only one of two ways: of the true God (approximately 1,400 times) or of a false god (6 times: Acts 7:43; 12:22; 28:6; 2 Cor. 4:4; Phil. 3:19; 2 Thess. 2:7). Whenever it is used of a false god, the context makes this very plain. To the list of instances referring to a false god some might wish to add two texts. The first is John 10:33, discussed above; as already explained, it cannot be interpreted to mean a genuine second god apart from the true God yet not a false god. The second text is Acts 17:23, where Paul refers to a pagan altar "to an unknown God" NWT. This can be understood to refer either to the true God (as seen from Paul's perspective) or to a false, pagan god (as worshiped by the Greeks), but again, not to "a god" which is neither the true God nor a false one. Thus there is no "third use" of the singular noun *theos* in the New Testament—either it is used of the true God or it is used of a false god in the context of idolatry of some sort.

Only if one assumes that the one case in which the "third use" is employed is with reference to Christ can such a third use be sustained. Not only does this assumption beg the question (that is, assume what is supposedly being proved), it has the decidedly unbiblical implication that there are two gods in the universe: "Jehovah God" and Jesus Christ—a "big God" and a "little god." By the JWs' count, this "third use" can be documented only three or at the most four times (John 1:1, 18, and perhaps 20:28; also John 10:33, already discussed). It is extremely unlikely that such a third use exists at all, therefore; it is far more likely—reasonably certain—that only the two uses exist, and therefore that the passages in John must be understood to be calling Jesus the true God.

## From HO THEOS to THEOS

We have argued that the shift from *ton theon* (the accusative form of *ho theos*) to the anarthrous *theos* in John 1:1 indicates a shift in nuance, such that the Word is called "God" in the fullest sense yet without identifying him as the person of God the Father. This argument requires that a shift from *ho theos* to *theos* in Scripture does not normally indicate a change in its basic meaning. On the other hand, the JWs' interpretation of John 1:1 crumbles further if it can be shown that normally such a shift within a short space does not indicate a major change of meaning.

With this in mind, the following passages are instructive:

| | |
|---|---|
| John 3:2 | ". . . you as a teacher have come from God [*apo theou*]; because no one can perform these signs that you perform unless God [*ho theos*] is with him." |
| John 13:3 | [Jesus] knowing . . . that He came forth from God [*apo theou*] and was going to God [*pros ton theon*] . . . |
| Rom. 1:21 | . . . although they knew God [*ton theon*], they did not glorify him as God [*theon*] . . . |
| 1 Thess. 1:9 | . . . how YOU turned to God [*pros ton theon*] from [your] idols to slave for a living and true God [*theō*]. |

Heb. 9:14 . . . how much more will the blood of Christ, who through an everlasting spirit offered himself without blemish to God [*to theō*], cleanse our consciences from dead works that we may render sacred service to [the] living God [*theō*]?

1 Peter 4:11–12 If anyone speaks, [let him speak] as it were [the] sacred pronouncements of God [*theou*]; if anyone ministers, [let him minister] as dependent on the strength which God [*ho theos*] supplies; so that in all things God [*ho theos*] may be glorified through Jesus Christ . . .

The above passages do not conform to the same syntax as the anarthrous predicate nominative uses of *theos* preceding the verb discussed earlier. However, they do serve as confirmatory evidence that a shift from *ho theos* to *theos* does not indicate a change in the meaning of the word.

### How Should John 1:1 Be Translated?

The question to which everything preceding has been leading is how the third clause of John 1:1 should be translated. As has already been explained, in another context "a God" might not be misunderstood as teaching a second, inferior deity (such as, Luke 20:38), but in John 1:1 such a translation would certainly carry that implication. We have also noted that translating "the Word was God" can give the misleading impression that the Word was God the Father, although certainly those who understand correctly the biblical teaching about God will not make that mistake.

It is likely, therefore, that no English translation is going to be immune from misunderstanding. Earlier we suggested that the entire verse might be translated, "In the beginning was the Word, and the Word was with the Deity, and the

Word was Deity." Were it not for the fact that in English we normally do not translate *theos* as "Deity," this translation might be the best possible.

Inevitably, the translation of this verse must depend to a certain extent on an understanding of the rest of the Bible. Taken out of its biblical context and transposed to a pagan Greek context, "the Word was a God" would be a possible rendering. However, in that context "God" in the preceding clause ("the Word was with God") would not refer to the God of the Bible, to a one true and almighty God. This is because, as has been conclusively demonstrated, grammatically *theos* refers to the Word as *theos* in the same sense as, or of the same kind as, *ton theon*. Thus, in a pagan context *ton theon* would refer to the same kind of "god" as *theos*— namely, a finite god in a pantheon of many gods. The point is that for JWs to translate "a god" is in one sense grammatically possible, but *only if they are willing to adopt a pagan interpretation of the entire verse*. It is completely invalid for them to translate the first two clauses in keeping with biblical theology, and then to translate the third clause in a way acceptable only to pagan polytheistic readers. In other words, it *is* grammatically impossible to understand *ton theon* in the second clause to mean an infinite, eternal, and absolutely unique Creator God, and in the third clause to understand *theos* to mean simply a mighty angel.

If the biblical use of the word *theos* is taken seriously, then, as we have shown, in the Bible the singular *theos* means either the true God or a false god of some sort. The JW interpretation allows for neither of these two possibilities in John 1:1, and so their translation, "the Word was a god," actually violates the biblical use of the singular *theos*.

Any translation of John 1:1, then, which is accurate, must be faithful to the following pieces of information.

1. There is only one genuine or real *theos*.
2. The Word was *theos* in the same sense as *ton theon*.

3. The Word is to be distinguished as somehow personally distinct from *ton theon*.

The only way to put these three facts together is to understand God as one God, yet existing as more than one person.
This is precisely what the doctrine of the Trinity asserts. (As
has already been explained, this does not mean that the Holy
Spirit needed to be mentioned here, since John's concern is
with the person of the Word, not with the Trinity as a whole
subject.) Thus, the person called "the God" in the second
clause is one person who is God, and the Word is a second
person who is God; yet these two persons are not two Gods
but one God.

The traditional translation "and the Word was God" is still
one of the clearest and most accurate renderings which
avoids paraphrasing. However, alternate renderings are possible which reflect this interpretation. "The Word was divine" is acceptable, as long as "divine" is understood as the
adjectival equivalent of "God." "The Word was deity" is perhaps less open to misunderstanding on this point but means
essentially the same thing. "The Word was God by nature" is
another way of communicating the idea. In any case, the
proper interpretation of John 1:1 rules out the JW doctrine of
the Word as a created angel and proves that in fact the Word
was a second person in the one Almighty God.

# 5

## Scholars' Words About the Word in John 1:1

U p to now, comparatively little reference has been made to the opinions of biblical scholars concerning John 1:1. An assumption which the author of this book shares with JWs is that the opinions of scholars are worth considering but they are not authoritative. For this reason, I have delayed sustained discussion of the treatment of John 1:1 in the scholarly literature until after a careful examination of the text itself.

At this point, then, it is appropriate to examine some of the more important scholarly treatments of John 1:1, especially those to which reference has been made in JW literature and in evangelical apologetic literature. The first of these is a highly influential article by E. C. Colwell.

### Colwell's Rule

In 1933, E. C. Colwell published an article in the *Journal of Biblical Literature* entitled (in an almost amusing play on words), "A Definite Rule for the Use of the Article in the Greek New Testament."[1] This article has occasioned much scholarly comment,[2] and is often mentioned in discussions about John 1:1.

Toward the beginning of his essay, Colwell defines his "rule" for sentences containing a predicate nominative and a

65

copula as follows: "A definite predicate nominative has the article when it follows the verb; it does not have the article when it precedes the verb."[3] Worded in that fashion, the rule might be misunderstood to be an inflexible one. However, Colwell later notes that there are exceptions to both halves of his rule; that is, that there are instances of definite predicate nominatives preceding the verb that have the article, and definite predicate nominatives following the verb that do not have the article.[4] Toward the end of the essay he concludes:

> The following rules may be tentatively formulated to describe the use of the article with definite predicate nouns in sentences in which the verb occurs. (1) Definite predicate nouns here regularly take the article. (2) The exceptions are for the most part due to a change in word-order: (a) Definite predicate nouns which follow the verb (this is the usual order) usually take the article; (b) Definite predicate nouns which precede the verb usually lack the article; (c) Proper names regularly lack the article in the predicate; (d) Predicate nominatives in relative clauses regularly follow the verb whether or not they have the article.[5]

Colwell's study has been accepted for over half a century now as a genuine contribution to the field of biblical Greek scholarship. A representative statement is that of Lane C. McGaughy in his 1970 doctoral dissertation (completed under Robert W. Funk, one of America's foremost Greek grammarians, whose dissertation was on the Greek article[6]):

> In a pioneer study of 1933, E. C. Colwell has conclusively demonstrated that such speculative statements [as that nouns with the article are definite while those without the article are indefinite, or that the use or nonuse of the article indicates various theological nuances, or that the fluctuation is merely stylistic], which are mainly based on private hunches, need not serve as the basis for a grammar of the article with predicate nominatives. Indeed, his work on the article in the predicates of S-II sentences [i.e., sentences with a subject noun, a linking verb, and a "subjective complement" or predicate

nominative] stands as a model of descriptive analysis for New Testament Greek studies.[7]

McGaughy goes on to comment,

> Although Colwell's study of all the occurrences of definite predicate nouns with a form of the equative verb revealed some exceptions, the overwhelming majority of examples conformed to the rule . . .[8]

These comments, while praising Colwell's study and agreeing with his conclusions, also point up one of the limitations of Colwell's rule: it is not an absolute rule but a useful generalization that holds in the vast majority of cases. It is thus a mistake to argue that Colwell's rule proves that *theos* in John 1:1 is definite, though if it were definite, Colwell's rule would explain why the article is absent. Furthermore, there is another limitation as well, one which many people who have cited Colwell's rule with respect to John 1:1 have failed to notice. Colwell's rule applies only to definite nouns; that is, it tells us something about when definite nouns will have the article and when they will not. It cannot, therefore, tell us whether a noun is definite or not. The reason for this is simply that the rule cannot be said to apply to a noun until after the noun has been determined to be definite. To argue that a noun must be definite because of Colwell's rule, therefore, is logically fallacious. That is, it would be fallacious to argue that merely because an anarthrous noun precedes the verb, it *must* be definite, as our analysis of such nouns in chapter 3 has demonstrated. This point has been well made by other writers.[9]

On the other hand, it is legitimate to argue that a noun cannot be proved indefinite merely because of the absence of the article. Colwell is therefore quite right when he states:

> They [the data presented in his study] show that a predicate nominative which precedes the verb cannot be translated as an indefinite or a "qualitative" noun solely because of the

absence of the article; if the context suggests that the predicate is definite, it should be translated as a definite noun in spite of the absence of the article. In the case of a predicate noun which follows the verb the reverse is true; the absence of the article in this position is a much more reliable indication that the noun is indefinite.[10]

Having made this point, which appears to be unassailable, Colwell then proceeds to draw a conclusion which many have since come to believe goes beyond the evidence of his own study:

Loosely speaking, this study may be said to have increased the definiteness of a predicate noun before the verb without the article, and to have decreased the definiteness of a predicate noun after the verb without the article.[11]

How can Colwell say this, when by his own admission his study was restricted to definite nouns? Is he not arguing illogically? Although it is possible to construe Colwell's statement as a logical blunder (which would not invalidate the rest of Colwell's fine article), in this writer's opinion it is better to take Colwell seriously when he qualifies his statement as "loosely speaking." That is, Colwell is *not* necessarily saying that an anarthrous predicate noun is most likely, as a matter of statistical measure, to be definite if it precedes the verb. Rather he is simply saying that we should be more readily prepared to acknowledge as definite those anarthrous predicate nouns that precede the verb where context does not demand them to be construed as indefinite. This seems to be a fair understanding of Colwell, as well as a proper approach to anarthrous predicate nouns, given the evidence which Colwell amassed in defense of his rule, as long as it is not abused.

Colwell's application of this conclusion to John 1:1, however, does appear to go beyond the evidence of his own study:

*Kai Theos ēn ho logos* looks much more like "And the Word was God" than "And the Word was divine" when viewed with reference to this rule. The absence of the article does *not* make the predicate indefinite or qualitative when it precedes the verb; it is indefinite in this position only when the context demands it. The context makes no such demand in the Gospel of John, for this statement cannot be regarded as strange in the prologue of the gospel which reaches its climax in the confession of Thomas [John 20:28].[12]

As we have seen, there is reason for regarding *theos* in John 1:1c as both indefinite and qualitative from the context (specifically Clause B). On the other hand, Colwell is right in saying that the mere absence of the article in Clause C cannot prove that *theos* is not definite. He also recognizes that his rule does not by itself prove that *theos* is definite. And it is not necessarily the case that a qualitative interpretation of *theos* would dictate the translation "divine." Where Colwell's rule can and has been severely abused is in the popular evangelical apologetic argument that the rule alone refutes the JW rendering "a god." Such an argument goes far beyond what Colwell himself, careful scholar that he was, said ("looks more like" is a far cry from "must be seen as").

While Colwell's rule cannot determine the correct translation of John 1:1, it is certainly not legitimate to dismiss Colwell's rule, as some otherwise knowledgeable JWs have done. For example, one JW—who has a master's degree in Greek and Latin, and should therefore know better—has in correspondence with this writer and other Christians derided Colwell's rule as "Colwell's dream" and "Colwell's fantasy."[13]

Yet, if Colwell's rule does not prove that *theos* in John 1:1 means "God," does that mean that "a god" is a legitimate translation? The answer to this question is emphatically *no* for the reasons given in the preceding chapters of this book.

## Harner on Qualitative Anarthrous Predicates

Forty years after Colwell's article appeared in the *Journal of Biblical Literature*, another article was published in that periodical on the subject of anarthrous predicate nouns. This one by Philip B. Harner was entitled "Qualitative Anarthrous Predicate Nouns: Mark 15:39 and John 1:1."[14] Harner reopened the question of whether or not *theos* in John 1:1 was "definite" (as Colwell had argued). Harner's conclusion: "In John 1:1 I think that the qualitative force of the predicate is so prominent that the noun cannot be regarded as definite."[15] This one sentence has been quoted by many JWs, including in official Watchtower publications, as proof that "the Word was a god" is a valid translation of John 1:1c.[16]

The JW reasoning here is that "qualitative" means that the noun takes on some sort of vague and weakened adjectival force, so that John 1:1 means only that "the Word was godlike, divine, a god."[17] In other words, the Word has *some* (not all) of the qualities or attributes of God, and possesses them to a *lesser degree* than God himself does. This allows the JWs to speak of Jesus as "divine" and "a god" while denying his omnipotence, eternality, and so forth.

The truth is that the JWs have misunderstood the term *qualitative* as used by Harner and other grammarians. Assuming the qualitative use of the anarthrous predicate noun preceding the verb applies in John 1:1, it is beyond dispute that this makes the Word "God" to the same degree or extent as the "God" with whom the Word existed (though not the same *person*). That is, in fact, Harner's own conclusion, based on what *he* meant by the term *qualitative*:

> Perhaps the clause could be translated, "the Word had the same nature as God." This would be one way of representing John's thought, which is, as I understand it, that *ho logos* ["the Word"], no less than *ho theos* ["the God"], had the nature of *theos*.[18]

That Harner's understanding of "qualitative" does not mean that Jesus is not called "God" in John 1:1 is clear from

his discussion of Rudolf Bultmann's interpretation of John
1:1, where he concludes:

> In terms of the analysis that we have proposed, a recognition
> of the qualitative significance of *theos* would remove some
> ambiguity in his [Bultmann's] interpretation by differentiating
> between *theos,* as the nature that the Logos shared with God,
> and *ho theos* as the "person" to whom the Logos stood in
> relation. Only when this distinction is clear can we say of the
> Logos that "he was God."[19]

In fact, Harner rules out the "a god" rendering. Setting
out five ways which John could have worded the final clause
of John 1:1, he labels these five clauses *A* through *E* (all of
which are variations of what in this book has been called
Clause C):[20]

A  *ho logos ēn ho theos*
B.  *theos ēn ho logos*
C.  *ho logos theos ēn*
D.  *ho logos ēn theos*
E.  *ho logos ēn theios*

Clause A, *ho logos ēn ho theos,* "would mean that *logos* and
*theos* are equivalent and interchangeable,"[21] so that the Word
was the person called "God" in the middle clause ("and the
Word was with God"). Besides making the sentence contradictory, this would mean that Jesus was the Father, as has
already been explained. This clause, then, would be incompatible both with the orthodox and the JW interpretation of
John 1:1.

Clause B, *theos ēn ho logos,* is what John actually wrote.
Clause C, *ho logos theos ēn,* would in Harner's view be
"identical in meaning" to Clause B "but differ slightly in
emphasis."

Clause D, *ho logos ēn theos,* "would probably mean that the
*logos* was 'a god' or a divine being of some kind, belonging to
the general category of *theos* but as a distinct being from *ho*

*theos.*" This is precisely the interpretation of John 1:1c held by the JWs; yet such an interpretation, according to Harner at least, would apply not to what John actually wrote but to a somewhat different statement.

Clause E, *ho logos ēn theios* (with the adjectival *theios* in place of the noun *theos*), "would mean that the logos was 'divine,' without specifying further in what way or to what extent it was divine. It could also imply that the *logos*, being only *theios*, was subordinate to *theos*." This clause then would also have been perfectly suited to convey the meaning of John 1:1 as understood by JWs; but John also did not choose this wording.

Harner then concludes, "John evidently wished to say something about the *logos* that was other than A *and more than D and E*" (my emphasis). In other words, John did not want to say that the Word was God the Father, the person with whom he existed in the beginning; nor did John want to say merely that the Word was "a god" or "divine"—he wanted to say *more* than that. Specifically, he wanted to say that the Word was just as much God, in terms of essence or nature, as "the God," that is, the Father.

The difference between B and C, according to Harner, is minimal, a difference of emphasis only. Both clauses would mean that "the *logos* has the nature of *theos*," but "C would mean that the *logos* (rather than something else) had the nature of *theos*. B means that the *logos* has the nature of *theos* (rather than something else)."

To use Harner's article in defense of the rendering "the Word was a god," then, betrays a complete misunderstanding of his article. He specifically rules out such a rendering by arguing that John would have written something different had he wished to be so understood. He also rules out the rendering "divine" for *theos* if "divine" is understood to imply that the *logos* is not *theos* in the same sense as *ho theos* (or *ton theon*) is in the preceding clause. (As we have already noted, Harner accepts the rendering "divine" if it is understood to mean "that the Word is 'divine' in the same sense that *ho theos* is divine."[22]) Therefore, Harner's article actually disproves the validity of the NWT rendering.

Before leaving Harner's article, it is worth looking at his conclusion. "Perhaps the clause could be translated, 'the Word had the same nature as God.' This would be one way of representing John's thought, which is, as I understand it, that *ho logos,* no less than *ho theos,* had the nature of *theos.*"[23] JWs have sometimes in conversations about John 1:1 argued that Harner's conclusion here could be dismissed on the basis of his qualifying words, "as I understand it." They have argued on the basis of these words that here Harner is giving us his own theological opinion, as distinguished from his scholarly, objective arguments in the preceding pages. But this is not at all correct. By "as I understand it" he clearly means "as I have been arguing throughout this article," or, "as the preceding evidence leads me to conclude." He has already drawn the same conclusion in the main analysis of the clause in question and is now simply repeating it.

Ironically the sentence which JWs tend to quote most often from Harner's article comes in the very next paragraph: "In John 1:1 I think the qualitative force of the predicate is so prominent that the noun cannot be regarded as definite." As we have already noted, the JWs mistakenly think that if *theos* in John 1:1 can be shown not to be definite they have won their case for the "a god" rendering. But what is ironic is the fact that Harner in this very sentence also qualifies his statement with the words "I think," yet the JWs quote this sentence as an authoritative scholarly word on the subject. The point is not that this sentence is in error; as has been argued, *theos* in John 1:1c is not definite, and if it were it would mean that the Word was God the Father. The point is that those JWs who have dismissed Harner's earlier (and more basic) conclusion because it was his opinion are thereby operating on a double standard to quote a statement by Harner qualified by "I think."

## Ernst Haenchen

An article in the December 15, 1985, issue of the *Watch-tower* (p. 25) quotes at length from the 1984 English transla-tion by Robert W. Funk[24] of the German scholar Ernst Haenchen's 1980 commentary on John,[25] to prove that John 1:1 does not teach that Jesus is God. This article is typical of the way in which JWs misuse scholarly citations in defense of their rendering of John 1:1.

According to Funk's translation, Haenchen would render the last clause of John 1:1, "and divine [of the category di-vinity] was the Logos."[26] Here, then, is a recent scholarly work rendering the anarthrous predicate *theos* as "divine" instead of "God." JWs understand this to mean that the Logos is, as Funk puts it, "of the category divinity," or, as the NWT says, "a god," but a god of a lesser sort than the God of the second clause of the verse *(ton theon)*. Thus, they take John 1:1 to mean that Jesus possesses a lesser form of deity than God himself, and claim Haenchen as support.

Ironically, something has been lost in the translation, not only of John, but also of Haenchen. His original German translation of John 1:1 reads, *"und Gott (von Art) war der Logos."*[27] Word for word, without regard for syntax, this reads, "and God (in essence) was the Logos,"[28] or, in correct English syntax, "and the Logos was (in essence) God." This, of course, is exactly the orthodox interpretation of John 1:1, according to which the Logos is just as much God in terms of essence or nature as *ton theon* in the second clause, but is to be distinguished as a different person from the person iden-tified as *ton theon*, that is, the Father. No doubt Funk was trying to bring out this same thought in his translation by rendering *theos* "divine." To most English-speaking biblical scholars, "divine" usually is nothing more nor less than an adjectival form of "God," and does not imply inferiority but rather equality of nature as compared to God himself. The Jehovah's Witnesses, however, use "divine" to refer to an inferior deity. This semantical confusion regularly results in the Jehovah's Witnesses misunderstanding the sources they cite to defend their interpretation of John 1:1.

The December 15, 1985, *Watchtower* article continues by quoting the following statement by Haenchen: "John 1:1, however, tells of something that was in existence already in time primeval; astonishingly, it is not 'God.'"[29] The Witnesses naturally seize on this statement as support for their belief that Jesus is not God. However, again they misunderstand Haenchen. What he means is that the subject of the first clause of John 1:1, the One who exists "in the beginning," is not identified merely as "God," but is called "the Logos." Thus, Haenchen actually says, "astonishingly, it is not 'the God' [*der Gott*],"[30] because he is talking about the identification of the subject of the sentence, not the meaning of the anarthrous *theos* in the last clause of the verse. Furthermore, in the very next sentence (which the *Watchtower* article omitted with an ellipsis), Haenchen writes, "The hymn [Haenchen regards John 1:1–18 as a Christian hymn] thus does not begin with God and his creation, but with the existence of the Logos in the beginning."[31] This proves that Haenchen was talking about John 1:1a, not John 1:1c.

Haenchen's next statement, quoted by the *Watchtower*, is as follows:

> The Logos (we have no word in either German or English that corresponds to the range of meaning of the Greek term) is thereby elevated to such heights that it almost becomes offensive. The expression is made tolerable only by virtue of the continuation in "and the Logos was in the presence of God," viz., in intimate, personal union with God.[32]

The *Watchtower* article then asks the rhetorical question (to which the assumed answer is *yes*), "Does that sound as if scholar Haenchen discerned in the Greek some distinction between God and the Logos, or Word?" The answer, of course, is *yes*, but in thinking that this rules out the trinitarian interpretation of John 1:1, the Jehovah's Witnesses have yet again misrepresented the doctrine of the Trinity. The question clearly implies that the Trinity makes no distinction between "God" and "the Word," whereas this is false: In John 1:1 "God" in the second clause is understood to be the Father, whereas "the Word" is the Son, not the Father.

The next paragraph in the *Watchtower* article quotes extensively from Haenchen regarding the difference between *theos* and *ho theos*. In Funk's translation of Haenchen's comments, he has Haenchen saying that *theos* meant "god, divine" whereas *ho theos* meant "God," and citing Philo and Origen as proof:

> In order to avoid misunderstanding, it may be inserted here that *theos* and *ho theos* ("god, divine" and "the God") were not the same thing in this period. Philo has therefore written: the *logos* means only *theos* ("divine") and not *ho theos* ("God") since the Logos is not God in the strict sense. Philo was not thinking of giving up Jewish monotheism. In a similar fashion, Origen, too, interprets: the Evangelist does not say the logos is "God," but only that the logos is "divine."[33]

Once again, Funk has inserted "divine" to interpret *theos*, but to make matters worse, he has also given "god" as a possible rendering. While in certain contexts the word *theos* can be translated "god" instead of "God," these are passages in which *theos* represents a false god, a meaning foreign to the context of John 1:1, as has already been explained. To render *theos* "god" automatically makes it refer to "a god" other than the biblical God, which is inconsistent with the monotheistic faith of the Scriptures. It might seem that Haenchen agrees with this erroneous interpretation, since he goes on to argue that the distinction between *theos* and *ho theos* is one of subordination, and that Paul's preincarnate Christ, like the Logos, is "such a divine being" *(ein solches gottliches Wesen),* existing "alongside and under God." However, things are not what they seem.

First of all, Haenchen uses the terms *divine being* and *entity* to mean nothing more nor less than what trinitarian theologians mean by "divine person." He is *not* arguing that the Logos is a second god of inferior nature. After citing Philippians 2:6–10 as another text where the preexistent Christ is viewed as a "divine being," Haenchen states,

> Thus, in both Philippians and John 1:1 it is not a matter of a dialectical relationship between two-in-one, but of a personal union of two entities, and to that personal union corresponds the church's rejection of patripassianism.[34]

Note that the *Watchtower* quoted this sentence, but omitted the last clause referring to patripassianism, without even using an ellipsis. In context, then, what Haenchen is refuting is not a trinitarian reading of John 1:1, but a modalistic one. In particular, he has his eye on Bultmann, who did characterize the relationship between the Logos and God as "dialectical."

Second, Haenchen goes on to argue that John 1:1a teaches that the Logos "existed before the creation and was not therefore created; it shared the highest of all distinctions with 'God, the Father' himself: the 'Logos' is eternal."[35] Of course, the Jehovah's Witnesses cannot accept this conclusion, because they teach that Christ is a created, temporal being; thus, they ignore Haenchen's comments on this point.

Third, Haenchen makes it clear that the subordination he is talking about is one of position or rank, not of essence or nature:

> But there was no rivalry between the Logos as *theos* and as *ho theos* (in English the distinction is expressed by "divine" and "God"); the new (Christian) faith does not conflict with the old monotheistic faith. That becomes clearer in verse 1c: "and divine (in essence) was the Logos." In this instance, the verb "was" (*ēn*) simply expresses predication. And the predicate noun must accordingly be more carefully observed: *theos* is not the same thing as *ho theos* ("divine" is not the same thing

as "God"). That contains a christology of the subordination of
the son, albeit still covertly. It is precisely for this reason that
the believer sees the Father in the son: the son does not speak
his own words, he does not do his own works, he does not
effect his own will, but subordinates himself entirely to the
words, work, and will of the Father.[36]

Once again, this passage is not cited in the *Watchtower*
article, because it undercuts the interpretation of John 1:1
which they are attempting to extract from Haenchen's commentary. They want Haenchen to say that the Logos is some
sort of demigod, a divine being of an inferior kind in comparison to the Almighty God. What Haenchen actually
means to say, though, is that the Logos is a divine person
existing from eternity in personal relationship with God the
Father, and that he is just as much *theos* as God himself!

One of the reasons why some of Haenchen's comments on
John 1:1 appear at first reading to support the Watchtower
doctrine of the Logos as a second god is that Haenchen does
not distinguish between definite, indefinite, and qualitative
uses of the noun. In fact, Haenchen takes no notice at all of
Harner's 1973 study of John 1:1 in the *Journal of Biblical Literature* which focused on this very issue.[37] What makes this so
surprising is that Haenchen's own German edition lists
nearly 150 references in his bibliography for John 1:1–18,
many of which are in English, and two of which are articles
in the *Journal of Biblical Literature* itself.[38] Nor does the bibliography in Funk's translation list Harner's excellent study.
Had Haenchen considered the arguments put forth by
Harner, he might have handled the distinction between *theos*
and *ho theos* a little better. Even so, Haenchen does set forth
an exegesis of John 1:1 that agrees in substance with the
trinitarian interpretation of that verse.

## William Barclay

In May 1977 *The Watchtower* defended their interpretation
of John 1:1 by citing from William Barclay's book *Many Witnesses, One Lord*,[39] where he does argue that in John 1:1 *theos*,

because it lacks the definite article, "becomes a description, and more of an adjective than a noun," and concludes that John "does not say that Jesus was God."[40] The *Watchtower* article, however, omitted these crucial remarks by Barclay in the same section:

> The only modern translator who fairly and squarely faced this problem is Kenneth Wuest, who said: "The Word was as to his essence essential deity." But it is here that the NEB [*New English Bible*] has brilliantly solved the problem with the absolutely correct rendering: "What God was the Word was."[41]

In a letter dated August 26, 1977, Barclay commented:

> The Watchtower article has, by judicious cutting, made me say the opposite of what I meant to say. What I was meaning to say, as you well know, is that Jesus is not the same as God, to put it more crudely, that he is of the same stuff as God, that is of the same being as God, but the way the Watchtower has printed my stuff has simply left the conclusion that Jesus is not God in a way that suits themselves.
>
> If they missed from their answer the translation of Kenneth Wuest and the N.E.B., they missed the whole point.[42]

To say that Jesus is "of the same being as God" is, of course, the same as the Athanasian Creed's statement that Christ is "of the same essence as the Father" (Greek, *homoousios tō patri*). Thus, when Barclay states that John "does not say that Jesus was God," he is simply making the common observation that by not saying "the Word was *the* God," John was avoiding identifying the Word as God the Father.

Even after Barclay's clear statement on the matter, the JWs continue to quote the same passage in exactly the same manner, omitting the reference to Wuest and the NEB.[43] This suggests that either they have still "missed the whole point," or that they do not care what Barclay meant as long as his words can be twisted to their own purpose.

### John L. McKenzie

Both Nelson Herle[44] and, evidently following his example, the Watchtower Society,[45] cite as support for their view of John 1:1 the following single sentence from John L. McKenzie's *Dictionary of the Bible:* "Jn 1:1 should rigorously be translated 'the word was with the God [= the Father], and the word was a divine being" (McKenzie's brackets).[46] Given the way in which the JWs use the word *divine*, one can certainly see how they might read this single sentence as consistent with their doctrine (although technically speaking they should object to McKenzie's use of the word "being" with reference to Christ, since in their view only God is a "being").

However, read in context, this sentence *must* be understood as affirming the orthodox trinitarian understanding of John 1:1, which, as we have explained, is that the Word was divine in the same sense that "God" in Clause B is divine, while remaining a second person distinct from the one called "God," that is, the Father. Even this one sentence contains some evidence that such was McKenzie's point, when after "God" he added in brackets, "the Father." The evidence becomes incontrovertible when the sentence is read in its larger context:

> The word *theos* is used to designate the gods of paganism. Normally the word with or without the article designates the God of the Old Testament and of Judaism, the God of Israel: Yahweh. But the character of God is revealed in an original way in the NT; the originality is perhaps best summed up by saying that God reveals Himself in and through Jesus Christ. The revelation of God in Jesus Christ does not consist merely in the prophetic word as in the OT, but in an identity between God and Jesus Christ. Jn 1:1–18 expresses this by contrasting the word spoken by the prophets with the word incarnate in Jesus. In Jesus the personal reality of God is manifested in visible and tangible form.

In the words of Jesus and in much of the rest of the NT the God of Israel *(ho theos)* is the Father of Jesus Christ. It is for this reason that the title *ho theos*, which now designates the Father as a personal reality, is not applied in the NT to Jesus Himself; Jesus is the Son of God (of *ho theos*). This is a matter of usage and not of rule, and the noun is applied to Jesus a few times. Jn 1:1 should rigorously be translated "the word was with the God [ = the Father], and the word was a divine being." Thomas invokes Jesus with the titles which belong to the Father, "My Lord and my God" (Jn 20:28). "The glory of our great God and Savior" which is to appear can be the glory of no other than Jesus (Tt [Titus] 2:13).[47]

The above requires little commentary. McKenzie states clearly that John 1:1–18 is speaking about "an identity between God and Jesus Christ" such that Jesus Christ is God "manifested in visible and tangible form." He explains that Jesus is not normally called *ho theos* only to avoid confusing him with the person of God the Father. He compares John 1:1 with Jesus being called "God" in John 20:28 and Titus 2:13. These statements form the context in which McKenzie says that the Word "was a divine being."

If that were not enough, on the same page McKenzie says that Yahweh (Jehovah) is a divine being! In his discussion of the name Yahweh, McKenzie writes:

This name needs no defining genitive; Yahweh is the God of Israel without further definition. The name implies that a *divine personal being* has revealed Himself as the God of Israel through the covenant and the exodus; it designates the *divine* personal reality as proclaimed and experienced [my emphasis].

With this piece of information, there can no longer be any doubt that in citing McKenzie the JWs have taken his words out of context and completely misconstrued his meaning.

## Other Scholars

The above discussions of John 1:1 as understood by E. C. Colwell, Philip B. Harner, Ernst Haenchen, William Barclay, and John L. McKenzie have been presented in some detail because these scholars are the ones currently being quoted in Watchtower literature. In the past, however, they have cited a number of other scholars. Nelson Herle has produced a large series of citations from scholarly reference works which he claims support the interpretation that John 1:1c means no more than that "the Word was a god."

Sorting through each and every one of these citations and discussing them in detail would double the length of this study. Fortunately this is unnecessary. For one thing, it is not our claim that no scholar has ever said anything that could be fairly construed as support for the JW interpretation of John 1:1. Rather, our claim is that *the facts* disprove the JW interpretation. We would add that the vast majority of trained biblical scholars have agreed, but that is not the basis for our conclusion. Furthermore, anyone caring to read in context the excerpted statements cited by Herle and the Watchtower publications will find the following to be the case: Either the statements have been misconstrued by being taken out of context (the usual situation), or in a few cases the person being cited is lacking in scholarly training, prejudiced against the doctrine of Christ's deity, or both.

Nevertheless, for the interested reader, some representative citations from recognized biblical scholars are here presented. Some of these are taken from some of the very sources quoted by the JWs to defend their interpretation of John 1:1. In light of the preceding study of that text, it should be evident that these sources have been misconstrued by the JWs.

**Henry Alford** (famed scholar of biblical Greek and ecclesiastical Latin):

> *Theos* must then be taken as implying *God, in substance and essence*—not *ho theos,* "the Father," *in person.* It does not = *theios,* nor is it to be rendered *a God*—but, as in *sarx egeneto* ["became flesh," John 1:14], *sarx* ["flesh"] expresses that *state*

into which the Divine Word entered by a definite act, so in *theos ēn* ["was God"], *theos* expresses that *essence* which was His *en archē* ["in the beginning"]:—that He was *very God*. So that this first verse might be connected thus: the Logos was from eternity,—was with God (the Father),—and was Himself God.[48]

## C. K. Barrett (prominent contemporary New Testament scholar):

The absence of the article indicates that the Word is God, but is not the only being of whom this is true; if *ho theos* had been written it would have implied that no divine being existed outside the second person of the Trinity.[49]

## C. H. Dodd (highly influential New Testament scholar; general director of the New English Bible translation committee):

On this analogy, the meaning of *theos ēn ho logos* will be that the *ousia* ["essence"] of *ho logos* ["the Word"], that which it truly is, is rightly denominated *theos* . . . That this is the *ousia* of *ho theos* (the personal God of Abraham, the Father) goes without saying. In fact, the Nicene *homoousios tō patri* ["of one essence with the Father"] is a perfect paraphrase.[50]

## Bruce Metzger (professor of Greek New Testament at Princeton; co-editor of the United Bible Societies' edition of the Greek New Testament):

It must be stated quite frankly that, if the Jehovah's Witnesses take this translation seriously, they are polytheists. . . . such a rendering is a frightful mistranslation.[51]

## James Moffatt (famous Bible translator, often cited by the JWs for his rendering of John 1:1 as "the Word was divine"):

"The Word was God. . . . And the Word became flesh," simply means "The Word was divine. . . . And the Word became human." The Nicene faith, in the Chalcedon definition, was intended to conserve both of these truths against theories that failed to present Jesus as truly God and truly man. . . .[52]

**A. T. Robertson** (prominent New Testament Greek scholar, author of massive Greek grammar textbook; frequently cited by JWs concerning John 1:1):

Winer, indeed, denies that the subject may be known from the predicate by its [the subject] having the article. But the rule holds wherever the subject has the article and the predicate does not. The subject is then definite and distributed, the predicate indefinite and undistributed. The word with the article is then the subject, whatever the order may be. So in Jo. 1:1, *theos ēn ho logos*, the subject is perfectly clear [i.e., *logos*].[53]

As a rule the article is not used with the predicate noun even if the subject is definite. The article with one and not with the other means that the articular noun is the subject. Thus *ho theos agapē estin* can only mean *God is love*, not *love is God*. So in Jo. 1:1 *theos ēn ho logos* the meaning has to be *the Logos was God*, not *God was the Logos*.[54]

**B. F. Westcott:**

The predicate ["God"] stands emphatically first, as in iv.24. It is necessarily without the article (*theos* not *ho theos*) inasmuch as it describes the nature of the Word and does not identify His Person. . . . No idea of inferiority of nature is suggested by the form of expression, which simply affirms the true deity of the Word.[55]

All of these biblical scholars (and the list could be extended for many pages) agree with the orthodox trinitarian interpretation of John 1:1, and for very good reasons, as this study has shown.

# Jesus as Jehovah in John 8:58

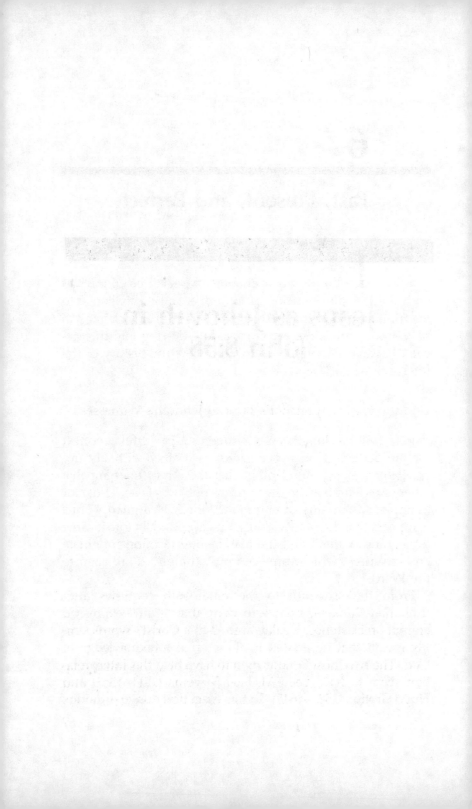

# 6

## Past, Present, and Perfect

In the next few chapters we shall be concerned with the JW interpretation of John 8:58 and its challenge to the trinitarian view that in that text Jesus implicitly claimed to be Jehovah, the Almighty God. Before delving into this debate, however, it will be useful to review the history of the interpretation of the verse.

### Unorthodox Interpretations Prior to Jehovah's Witnesses

John 8:58 has long been regarded as a powerful prooftext for the deity of Christ. For centuries it stood virtually unchallenged as scriptural proof that the Arian teaching that "there was a time when the Son was not" was false. Thus, for example, Athanasius, after quoting John 8:58, argued, "Thus it appears that the phrases 'once was not,' and 'before it came to be,' and 'when,' and the like, belong to things originate and creatures, which came out of nothing, but are alien to the Word."[1]

From the sixteenth to the nineteenth centuries antitrinitarian thinkers, unable to deny that "I am" expressed eternal preexistence, weakly argued that Christ's words simply meant that he existed in the eternal foreknowledge of God. The two most famous men to have held this interpretation seem to have been Michael Servetus (1511–1553) and Hugo Grotius (1583–1645). To this exegetical dodge orthodox scholars repeatedly replied that the same thing could be said by any human being. Calvin's response to Servetus was typical:

> I am quite aware of the captious argument with which erring spirits corrupt this passage: that he was before all ages because he was already foreknown as Redeemer, both in the Father's plan and in the minds of the godly. But since he clearly distinguishes the day of his manifestation from his eternal essence, and expressly commends his own authority as excelling Abraham's in antiquity, there is no doubt that he is claiming for himself what is proper to his divinity.[2]

Another antitrinitarian explanation of influence was that of Faustus Socinus (1539–1604), who with his uncle founded the theological movement known as Socinianism. According to Socinus, what Jesus was trying to say was something like this: "Before Abraham becomes Abraham [i.e., "father of many nations"], I am the Messiah," that is, Jesus must be the Messiah before Abraham can become the father of many nations. This interpretation simply ignored the actual wording of John 8:58, notably interpreting the past tense "came to be" (*genesthai*) as if it were future tense, and so was never widely accepted. As it was all too easy to show from the context that Jesus' claim was more than a claim to being the Messiah (8:59), the heretical explanation fell into disrepute[3] and the text became again an unanswerable prooftext for the deity of Christ.

In the twentieth century, the only scholarly rejection of the plain meaning of the text (that Jesus was claiming eternal preexistence and therefore deity) has come from scholars who argue that John's gospel does not give us an accurate report of the words of Jesus. A notable example is the argument of J. Ernest Davey, who writes:

> In John 8:58 we have probably a deliberate change of tense, i.e., from a claim of preexistence as Messiah to a claim of

divinity, made however in the Greek and due to the evangelist, who has also in other places in *John* interpreted words of Jesus in a mistaken way. . . .[4]

This argument rests on the long-refuted notion that the fourth gospel was written in the second century and represents a Hellenization of the message of Jesus.[5] Those scholars who hold fast to the inerrancy of Scripture agree that in John 8:58 Jesus claimed to be eternal.

## Jehovah's Witnesses' Interpretation

The JWs, however, deny the deity of Christ while confessing the inerrant authority of the Bible; consequently, they must interpret Jesus' words in this crucial text in some other way. A serious effort to deal with this problem began in 1950 with the publication of the first edition of the NWT. Since then, John 8:58 has become a major focal point of contention between orthodox Christian apologists and JWs. Indeed, the JWs' efforts to reinterpret John 8:58 to fit a nontrinitarian doctrine of Christ constitute the most serious challenge ever to the orthodox interpretation of this classic text.

A literal translation of Jesus' words would be, "Amen, Amen, I say to you, Before Abraham came into existence, I am" *(amēn, amēn, legō humin, prin Abraam genesthai, egō eimi).* As was the case with John 1:1, the Greek text of John 8:58 is not in dispute here; in the case of John 8:58, nor is the literal meaning of the words. Both the text and a literal rendering can be found in the JWs' own *Kingdom Interlinear Translation,*[6] where *egō eimi* is translated "I am."

To make John 8:58 appear to harmonize with their doctrine, the NWT renders Jesus' words, "Before Abraham came into existence, I *have been* (italics mine)." Why is this significant? For one thing, it eliminates any apparent allusion to Exodus 3:14 and the "I am" passages in Isaiah. It also softens the contrast between the two verbs ("came into existence"

and "am"), and in so doing enables the Witnesses to understand Jesus to mean that he simply existed some time prior
to Abraham without being eternally preexistent.

It should not be thought, however, that the issue is merely
a matter of translation. Several twentieth-century biblical
translators and scholars have rendered *eimi* with some form
of the English past tense, while at the same time insisting
that what was meant was eternal preexistence. Indeed, no
biblical scholar has ever rendered *eimi* in the past tense and
argued on that basis that the words did not indicate eternal
preexistence. The issue, then, as with John 1:1, is not merely
translation, but interpretation, although translation should
reflect interpretation and be guided by it.

JWs employ two basic kinds of arguments to defend their
"I have been" rendering. The first is an argument from pre-
cedent: other translators and scholars have rendered John
8:58 in this way, thus legitimizing such a rendering.[7] While
the fact that scholarly translators have rendered John 8:58 in a
similar manner suggests that the rendering is worthy of con-
sideration, it does not, of course, prove it to be valid, nor
does it prove that the interpretation adopted by the JWs is
valid. It is unfortunate but true that JWs lean far too often on
this approach to justify their unorthodox interpretations.

## Grammatical Arguments

The second is an argument from grammar: the words *egō
eimi*, although in the present tense, ought to be translated in
the perfect tense because of the grammatical context. The
exact form of the grammatical argument used has changed
two or three times since the 1950 NWT, in which the following footnote to John 8:58 appeared:

> I have been = *egō eimi (e.gō' ei.mi')* after the aorist infinitive
> clause *prin Abraam genesthai* and hence properly rendered in
> the perfect indefinite tense.[8]

Evangelical scholars were immediately critical of this footnote; representative was the criticism expressed by Walter
Martin, who wrote:

It is difficult to know what the author of the note on page 312 means since he *does not* use standard grammatical terminology, nor is his argument documented from standard grammars. . . . The term "perfect indefinite" is an invention of the author of the note, so it is impossible to know what is meant. . . .[9]

One might have expected that at this point the Society would have attempted to back up its footnote with documentation. If Martin's accusations were false, it would have been in the JWs' best interest for them to have shown that they *did* use "standard grammatical terminology," and that they did *not* invent the term "perfect indefinite."

Instead, the Society simply ignored the criticism, and presented a completely new defense of the rendering. In 1957, a *Watchtower* "Questions from Readers" on John 8:58 made no attempt to defend the term *perfect indefinite*—in fact, the term is not even mentioned. Instead, the article argued that "the Greek verb *eimi* must be viewed as a historical present."[10] However, historical presents have nothing to do with perfect tenses, nor with the present tense following an "aorist infinitive clause." Thus a new defense was introduced that in effect rejected the old one but was itself no better.

Later editions of the NWT retained the same footnote to John 8:58 with one change: the last three words of the first sentence (quoted above) were changed from "perfect indefinite tense" in the 1950 edition to "perfect tense indicative,"[11] "perfect indicative,"[12] or just "perfect tense."[13] The significance of this change will also be examined in this chapter, as it has a bearing on the issue of the meaning of the disputed expression, "perfect indefinite tense."

In 1978 Nelson Herle began distributing letters and papers defending, among other things, the NWT rendering of John 8:58 and the 1950 NWT footnote on that verse. Unlike the Watchtower Society itself, Herle attempted to show that the term *perfect indefinite tense* was a valid grammatical term. He argued further that the terms *perfect indefinite tense* and *perfect tense indicative* were roughly synonymous.

Herle also tried to show that the aorist clause preceding the present tense verb *eimi* did indeed require that *eimi* be interpreted as a perfect tense. Unlike the 1957 *Watchtower*, however, he did not appeal to the Greek idiom of the historical present, but to the idiom of the "present of past action still in progress." This idiom appears where a Greek present tense verb is used to describe an action which began in the past and continues to the present. Herle set forth this argument also in his 1983 unpublished book *The Trinity Doctrine*.[14]

In 1984, a reference edition of the NWT appeared with an appendix using the same argument in defense of the rendering "I have been" as Herle used in his book, based on the present of past action still in progress. The appendix did not, however, comment on the 1950 NWT use of the term *perfect indefinite tense*. It also avoided, as did Herle, any mention of the historical present.

### Which Defense?

It would seem, then, that the Watchtower Society has used at least three different defenses of the rendering "I have been" in John 8:58. In these three defenses, *eimi* follows an aorist infinitive clause and therefore (1) should be rendered in the perfect indefinite tense; (2) is an historical present; (3) is a present of past action still in progress.

The first of these arguments is rather general—it tells us that the aorist infinitive clause preceding *eimi* is grounds for rendering the present tense verb as a perfect, but it does not tell us why. The second and third arguments are more specific, appealing to two different idiomatic uses of the present tense in Greek as requiring a perfect tense rendering in English. These last two explanations, therefore, are contradictory to each other. That this is the case shall become clearer as each is examined in turn.

Given that the Society has offered two incompatible defenses of their rendering of John 8:58, the faithful JW will have no trouble deciding which to uphold: the latter. This is because the Witnesses are taught that the light of Bible doctrine emanating from the Society is growing progressively brighter, and that they should disregard "old light" where it is superseded by "new light."[15]

Yet the question must be asked why the Society would give a different reason for its rendering in 1984 than it gave in 1957. If they had a good reason for the rendering in 1950 when the translation first appeared, presumably they knew it then. Indeed, presumably the writer of the 1957 *Watchtower* article had a better chance of knowing that reason than the writer of the 1984 NWT appendix on John 8:58, since he was twenty-seven years closer to the source. Thus, whereas theologically the Witness may prefer to adhere to the 1984 explanation, the 1957 defense is historically more likely to be the translators' real basis. If it is claimed (as this writer has been told by Witnesses) that the reasoning of the translators in 1950 is now unknown, then it cannot be claimed that the argument presented in the 1984 NWT represents that reasoning. Instead, it becomes simply a justification after the fact.

## Indefinite and Indicative

As noted earlier in this chapter, the footnote to John 8:58 in the NWT was changed in later editions, so that the term *perfect indefinite tense* was altered to "perfect tense indicative," "perfect indicative," or simply "perfect tense." What is the significance of these changes?

According to JWs, the changes were simply a matter of using more commonly understood terminology. Specifically, they claim that the term *perfect indefinite tense* had been misunderstood to be a Greek tense rather than an English tense, and that the changes were made to clear up this misunderstanding. Thus, in a letter of February 7, 1978, to Firpo W. Carr, a JW, the Society stated: "The change was made in order to make it clearer that the footnote pertained to the English rendering rather than to the tense in the original Greek."[16]

This explanation, however, does not fit the facts. It is true that some Christian scholars have criticized the NWT footnote on the grounds that there is no such thing in Greek as the perfect indefinite tense.[17] And it may be, as Nelson Herle has argued, that the expression "rendered in" in that footnote should be understood to refer to the tense of the English rendering, although for many years JWs commonly defended it as a Greek tense.[18] But these points do not explain the change in the footnote in question. Changing "perfect indefinite tense" to "perfect tense indicative" does absolutely nothing to clarify that "rendered in" means rendered into English! If that is what the Society wished to clarify, all they had to do was add the words "into English." Unless we assume that the persons responsible for the revised footnote were utterly inept, it is inconceivable that what they were trying to do was to clarify that an English tense was meant.

Another explanation, this one offered by Herle, is that the Society realized that "perfect indefinite" was an unusual term, and so they simply decided to use more common terminology. Thus, he argues that the two expressions are synonymous:

> Whether one calls the tense the "perfect," "perfect indefinite," or "perfect tense indicative," all mean basically the same thing, "an event of past time." The terms "perfect" and "perfect tense indicative" are more common than "the perfect tense indefinite" and have been used in more recent editions of the NWT for the sake of using a more *common* term, not a more correct one.[19]

Herle's explanation fares no better than the Society's. It overlooks the fact, known to all first-year students of Greek, that "indicative" is a term describing the *mood* of the verb, while "indefinite," as used in the 1950 NWT footnote, is a term describing the *tense* of the verb. The indicative mood is simply that aspect of the verb that identifies it as a statement (rather than a question, command, or wish). Thus, it is simply not true that "perfect tense indicative" is synonymous with "perfect indefinite tense."

That Herle did not understand the difference can be seen from his use of the expression *perfect tense indefinite* as if it were identical to "perfect indefinite tense." The word *indefinite* following immediately after "perfect" and before "tense" is used to modify the word *perfect:* that is, this is not just any perfect tense, and it is not the perfect definite tense—it is the perfect *indefinite* tense. When, however, the word *indefinite* is placed after the word *tense,* it no longer functions as a modifier of the word *perfect.*

Since the mood of the verb *eimi* is not an issue in the debate over the meaning of John 8:58, and since it has nothing to do with rendering "I have been" rather than "I am," it would seem that there was no legitimate reason why the word *indicative* should have been added at all. What possible reason can be given? The simplest explanation, and the only one which makes sense of the facts, is that *indicative* was used because it looks and sounds similar to the word *indefinite.* To the casual reader, "indefinite" and "indicative" would appear so similar that he might not even notice the change; while the uninformed reader who did notice it would probably assume (as did Nelson Herle) that the two words were synonymous. Since the vast majority of Jehovah's Witnesses and their contacts are uninformed on such matters, the change was a shrewd one.

## The Perfect Indefinite Tense

The fact that the Watchtower Society dropped the term *perfect indefinite tense* and used similar-sounding terms in its place in later footnotes to John 8:58 suggests that they were unable to defend the former expression. As was pointed out

earlier, it is strange that the Society has never documented
the perfect indefinite tense from grammar textbooks if they
knew it could be so documented. This silence alone, of
course, cannot prove that the Society invented the term (as
such a "proof" would be an argument from silence). However, we have more than silence on which to base this
claim—we have the Society's own statement on the matter.
In their letter to Firpo Carr cited earlier, they explained the
use of the term as follows:

> What was meant was that the Greek present indicative *e.gō'*
> *ei.mi'* is here *rendered into English* in the perfect tense, "I have
> been," with an idea of indefiniteness. That is to say, no men-
> tion of the length of Jesus' prehuman existence is here
> given.[20]

Here the Society explicitly declares the reason for the term
*indefinite*. It served to communicate their belief that the word
*eimi*, while admittedly indicating the preexistence of Christ,
does not indicate "the length of Jesus' prehuman existence."
This is decidedly different from saying that there actually is a
perfect indefinite tense in English.

Despite this positive piece of evidence that the expression
*perfect indefinite tense* was coined by the author of the 1950
NWT footnote, Nelson Herle has for several years maintained
that the Society was using "standard grammatical terminology" (to use Walter Martin's phrase). He bases this claim
on two textbooks of English grammar. The first is *Crowell's
Dictionary of English Grammar and of American Usage*, by
Maurice H. Weseen, published in 1928; the second, *A New
English Grammar Logical and Historical*, by Henry Sweet, was
published in 1900.[21]

First of all, these two textbooks alone cannot document
that something is "standard grammatical terminology." In
order for them to do that, they would themselves have to be
standards in their fields—that is, books which have been
widely known and used, which have been reprinted over a

long period of time, and which have been well received by professionals in the field. By these criteria, neither Weseen's book nor Sweet's are standard English grammar textbooks.

Moreover, Weseen is dependent on Sweet for the terms *indefinite* and *definite* as applied to tense. Thus, Weseen writes, "*Definite Tense.* Sweet uses this term . . . Opposed to *Indefinite tense.* . . ."[22] The fact that Herle could find only these two textbooks, the most recent of which was published in 1928, and that one is dependent on the other for the term in question, indicates that the two books cited by Herle, even if they use the term *perfect indefinite tense,* cannot be used to establish it as standard terminology. Even Herle agrees that the term is not "common."[23]

Chart 1

|  | Indefinite | Definite |
|---|---|---|
| *Present* | I see. | I am seeing. |
| *Preterite* | I saw. | I was seeing. |
| *Perfect* | **I have seen.** | **I have been** seeing. |
| *Pluperfect* | I had seen. | I had been seeing. |
| *Future* | I shall see. | I shall be seeing. |
| *Future Perfect* | I shall have seen. | I shall have been seeing. |
| *Preterite Future* | I should see. | I should be seeing. |

Of course, if these two books do use the term, then it would seem that the Watchtower Society can be acquitted of the charge of making it up. This would be the case, though, only if the Society used the term in the same manner as the two books define and use it. This is not the case, however. Note table 1, found in both Weseen's and Sweet's books,[24] and reproduced by Nelson Herle[25] as evidence in favor of the perfect indefinite tense. From this chart it can be easily seen that Weseen and Sweet would indeed admit the use of the expression *perfect indefinite tense* in English grammar. According to this chart, as Herle points out, an example of the perfect indefinite would be "I have seen." This looks and sounds like an exact parallel to "I have been," the phrase used in the NWT at John 8:58. It would thus seem that Herle has produced the documentation for the perfect indefinite tense which the Society itself has failed to produce for thirty-five years.[26]

However, a closer look at the chart reveals something else. The exact phrase *I have been* occurs on the chart as part of the perfect *definite*, rather than the perfect indefinite. In this case, the perfect definite is "I have been seeing." Looking up the chart, we see that "I have been" would be the perfect definite of "I am." It would appear, then, that "I have been" is the perfect definite, not the "perfect indefinite," as the NWT footnote had said.

Perhaps it will be objected that the chart does not have "I have been" standing on its own. That is true, of course, but that is because "I have been," like "I am," always implies some sort of predicate ("I have been running"; "I have been here"; "I have been a teacher," and so forth). This is true, even if the words are taken to be an expression of existence, in which case the predicate "existing" is implied ("I have been existing"). Since "I have been existing" would be defined by Weseen and Sweet as the perfect definite, and since "existing" is the implied predicate of John 8:58 according to the interpretation of both orthodox Christians and the Jehovah's Witnesses, the conclusion cannot be avoided: "I have been" is the perfect definite, not the perfect indefinite.

What this implies, of course, is that it is highly unlikely that the Society had actually drawn from Weseen or Sweet in using the term *perfect indefinite tense;* and if they did, that would not say much for their scholarship, since they would have used it incorrectly.

In response, a JW might say that what matters is not whether this particular term was used correctly, but whether their interpretation is correct. Although such a response would to some extent be valid, yet it is relevant to note that JWs have exhibited poor scholarship in their handling of the term "perfect indefinite tense." Still, it is the interpretation of John 8:58 itself with which we are primarily concerned, and to which we will turn in the next chapters.

# 7

## Jesus Christ: Eternal, or Just Very Old?

According to the traditional interpretation of John 8:58, in that verse Jesus made a direct claim to being eternal. It was not simply that he was older than Abraham, although his statement says that much too, but that his existence is of a different kind than Abraham's—that Abraham's existence was created and finite, beginning at a point in time, while Christ's existence never began, is uncreated and infinite, and therefore eternal. The JWs cannot allow such an interpretation to go unchallenged, since it would prove that Jesus claimed implicitly to be God. They have therefore sought desperately over the years to find a grammatically based interpretation of John 8:58 that would remove the idea of eternal preexistence and make Jesus simply a very old figure in history.

### The Historical Present

As has already been noted, the 1957 article in the *Watchtower* dealing with John 8:58 stated that "in view of its being preceded by the aorist infinitive clause which refers to Abraham's past, the Greek verb *eimi'* must be viewed as a historical present."[1] Several JWs in Southern California have admitted privately to this author and to others as well that the *Watchtower* was wrong on this point, and so was Nelson Herle.[2] Moreover, none of the Society's books or magazines have mentioned the historical present in connection with John 8:58 since the 1957 *Watchtower* article.

It would seem, then, that the Witnesses are unable to defend this interpretation of John 8:58. However, the Society has yet to admit in print that they made a mistake. This makes it difficult to accept their claim that although they have made mistakes in the past, they freely admit them.[3] In fact, at the end of the 1978 letter to Firpo Carr already cited, the Society referred Carr for "further comments . . . to what has been published under 'Questions from Readers' in the February 15, 1957, issue of *The Watchtower*. . . ."[4] Evidently, then, the Society still stands by what they said in that article.

The article in question was unable to cite any scholarly writings of any kind in support of their claim that John 8:58 was an historical present. Instead, they simply quoted definitions and illustrations of the idiom from two textbooks in Greek grammar, Hadley and Allen's *Greek Grammar* and A. T. Robertson's massive *Grammar*. Ironically, these two sources themselves disprove that John 8:58 is an historical present, sometimes in the very words quoted by *The Watchtower*! The following points prove beyond reasonable doubt that the historical present is irrelevant to John 8:58.

1. The historical present is an idiom in which past events are narrated, story-telling fashion, in the present tense, as a vivid, dramatic way of projecting the reader or listener into the narrative. In John 8:58, on the other hand, Jesus' words do not tell a story or describe a past event, but instead simply state a comparison between Abraham and Jesus.

All of the Greek grammars agree on this understanding of the historical present. Hadley and Allen are cited by the *Watchtower* itself as stating that the idiom is used "in vivid narration."[5] Robertson agrees.[6] Some grammars distinguish between the historical present used in records (sometimes called the "annalistic" use) and that used in narratives (usually called the "dramatic"); a few divide the dramatic between historical narratives and reports of dreams and visions.[7] According to Robertson, the New Testament uses the dramatic form of the historical present[8]; but in any case, Christ's words in John 8:58 do not fit any of these categories of historical presents.

This idiom is common in all languages, including English; *Funk and Wagnalls Standard Desk Dictionary* defines it as "the present tense used to narrate a past event."[9] In English it is most common in conversation, not writing. Robert Funk gives the following sentence as an example: "Then these guys come in, see, and I says to them, 'Where do you think you're going?'"[10] In both Greek and English, then, the historical present is defined and used in the same way. There simply is no valid way to define historical presents to include John 8:58.

2. The historical present has nothing whatsoever to do with following an "aorist infinitive clause." The key statement in the *Watchtower* article is that "in view of its being preceded by the aorist infinitive clause which refers to Abraham's past, the Greek verb *eimi'* must be viewed as a historical present." This statement appears to mean that present tenses preceded by "aorist infinitive clauses" must by some rule of Greek grammar be translated in the past tense, because such constructions are examples of the historical present. At the very least, the statement means that a present tense verb following a past tense verb is an historical present.

Such an argument is proved false by the article itself. Hadley and Allen are again quoted as saying, "The present in this use is freely *interchanged* with the past tenses."[11] The article also cites John 1:29–42, John 20, and Mark 1:12–13 as "examples of where the Greek *mixes* the historical present with past tenses."[12] John 1:29 begins (translating literally), "The next day he beholds [*blepei*] Jesus coming toward him, and he says [*legei*]. . . ." In this verse there is no past tense verb preceding either of the two historical presents. Sometimes past tense verbs *follow* the historical presents, sometimes they precede them, and sometimes the historical presents stand alone.

In short, the presence of a past tense verb has absolutely nothing to do with the historical present. In trying to draw such a connection, the Watchtower Society has simply redefined the term *historical present* to suit themselves. Such a practice is indefensible, and unfortunately the JWs engage in this practice all too frequently.

These two points are enough to prove beyond reasonable doubt that identifying John 8:58 as an instance of the use of the historical present is in error. But there are some additional considerations which, while none of them are conclusive by themselves, serve to add further confirmation.

3. A check of some dozen Greek grammars and over sixty commentaries and studies on the Gospel of John shows that not one identifies John 8:58 as an historical present, or defines the idiom in such a way as to include that verse.

4. The historical present, according to C. F. Burney's list,[13] occurs 164 times in John. Yet in chapters 7–10 the historical present is used only six times, five of these with the verb *legei* ("he says") or its plural *legousin* ("they say"). The sixth occurrence is *agousin* ("they lead") in John 9:13. These figures do not prove that John 8:58 could not contain an historical present, but they do suggest that it is less likely.

5. None of the 164 historical presents listed by Burney use the verb *eimi* or any of its forms. Three-fourths of the historical presents occur with *legei* or *legousin*. None of the dozen grammars consulted give any examples of the historical present with *eimi*. Indeed, it has been asserted that *eimi* never occurs in the New Testament as an historical present.[14] Since the historical present is used to heighten the vividness of narration, it makes sense that the verb for "to be" would not occur as an historical present.

6. Finally, the historical present is used regularly in a punctiliar (or aoristic) sense, not in a durative sense,[15] whereas *eimi* in John 8:58 is indisputably durative. It is true that Robertson does allow for occasional durative uses of the historical present,[16] but unfortunately he gives no examples. None of the historical presents in John are durative. Burney

does list *phanei* in John 1:5 as an historical present, and *phanei* there is clearly durative; however, Burney also admits that it "may be open to dispute" whether it is an historical present at all. Since most translations (including the NWT) render *phanei* in the present tense, and in context John is not engaged in narration, John 1:5 may be ruled out as an historical present. Therefore, it can be confidently said that there are no durative historical presents at least in John, which militates against the notion that in John 8:58 *eimi* is an historical present.

There is thus no reason whatsoever to believe that *eimi* in John 8:58 is an historical present, and every reason to believe that it is not. This defense of the NWT rendering is so indefensible that Nelson Herle does not even mention it in his writings, not even in *The Trinity Doctrine*, where he spends over eight pages discussing John 8:58. Nor is it mentioned in any of the half a dozen or so discussions of the verse which have appeared in Watchtower publications since that 1957 *Watchtower* article.

## Present of Past Action in Progress

Since the late 1970s, Jehovah's Witnesses have begun using a different line of reasoning to defend their unorthodox interpretation of John 8:58. The first Witness to use this new argument was apparently Nelson Herle. In a 1978 letter to Walter Martin, after listing eleven translations (including the NWT) that render *eimi* in John 8:58 with some form of the past tense, Herle argued as follows:

> The Greek has a tense which is not found in the English: that tense which denotes action which began in the past and is still in progress. This tense is stated in the present tense and should be translated or rendered in the English perfect or as some still say the past tense. The above translations of John 8:58 are examples of this.[17]

A similar statement appeared in *The Trinity Doctrine*.[18] Both of these writings cited various Greek grammarians, in particular G. B. Winer and Nigel Turner, both of whom identified John 8:58 as an example of this particular idiom. Then in

1984 the Watchtower Society for the first time published a
discussion of John 8:58 using the same argument; it appeared in an appendix to the 1984 Reference Edition of the
NWT,[19] and was reprinted in the 1985 revision of the Society's
*Kingdom Interlinear Translation.*[20] Like Herle, the Society's
publications cited Winer and Turner as scholarly support.

It must be admitted that at least in this argument the
Witnesses are not completely without scholarly backing in
identifying John 8:58 as an instance of the present of past
action still in progress (hereafter abbreviated "PPA").[21] However, this fact does not at all help to establish their position on
the meaning of John 8:58. As we shall see, it is entirely
possible to identify *eimi* in John 8:58 as a PPA without implying that Jesus' words are not an assertion of eternal preexistence. Moreover, there are some important reasons to doubt
that John 8:58 is a PPA at all.

What exactly is the PPA, and what significance does it
have in the exegesis of this verse? We may begin by citing the
definitions given by Winer and Turner themselves. According to Winer:

> Sometimes the Present includes also a past tense
> (Mdv. 108), viz. when the verb expresses a state which com-
> menced at an earlier period but still continues,—a state in its
> duration. . . .[22]

And according to Turner:

> The Present which indicates the continuance of an action
> during the past and up to the moment of speaking is virtually
> the same as Perfective, the only difference being that the ac-
> tion is conceived as still in progress. . . .[23]

According to these grammarians, then, the PPA is essentially an idiomatic use of the present tense to speak of a state
or action which was occurring in the past and has continued
to occur up to the time of the speaker. In that limited and
general sense it may be agreed that John 8:58 is an instance of

such a usage of the present tense: Jesus certainly existed in the past, and he was existing at the time he uttered the words recorded in John. However JWs seek to find more in the idiom. They wish to argue that the use of this idiom does not permit orthodox Christians to claim with any certainty that Jesus was here asserting eternal preexistence.[24] Some, such as Nelson Herle,[25] even go so far as to claim that this idiom presupposes a beginning to the state described by the verb, since Winer speaks of the state as "commenced," and Burton speaks of it as "beginning in past time,"[26] thus proving that Jesus was in fact a created being.

The first point of importance to note is that Winer and Turner, the only two Greek grammarians known to include John 8:58 as an instance of the PPA, omit one very important fact about this particular idiom. Most grammars specifically state that accompanying the present tense verb is some adverbial expression indicating the extent of the duration of the time indicated by the verb. Thus Burton says that it is "accompanied by an adverbial expression denoting duration and referring to past time"[27]; Goodwin notes that it occurs "with *palai* or any other expression of past time"[28]; Dana and Mantey say that it "is generally associated with an adverb of time"[29]; and Robertson states, "Usually an adverb of time (or adjunct) accompanies the verb."[30]

This important qualification can be better understood by considering how this idiom occurs elsewhere in the New Testament. According to the various grammars already cited, the following passages (other than John 8:58) are examples of the PPA: Luke 2:48; 13:7; 15:29; John 5:6; 14:9; 15:27; Acts 15:21; 2 Cor. 12:19; 2 Tim. 3:15; 2 Peter 3:4; 1 John 2:9; 3:8. All but three of these texts (2 Tim. 3:15; 2 Peter 3:4; 1 John 2:9) are listed as examples of the idiom by the appendix on John 8:58 in the 1984 edition of the NWT.[31] An examination of these texts reveals that John 8:58 does not quite belong to this category of usage.

To begin with, two of these texts are usually and properly rendered in English as present tenses. First John 2:9 reads,

"He that says he is in the light and yet hates his brother is
[*estin*] in the darkness up to right now" (NWT; cf. KJV, NIV,
NEB, and others). Second Peter 3:4 quotes scoffers as saying,
". . . Why, from the day our forefathers fell asleep [in death],
all things are continuing [*diamenei*] exactly as from creation's
beginning" (NWT; cf. KJV, NIV, NEB, and others). In both of
these texts, the present tense verbs could have been rendered by the English perfect, but they *need not* have been, as
the NWT itself demonstrates. It is simply untrue, therefore,
that the PPA *must* be rendered in a past tense; it may be, but
need not be. It is also obviously untrue that the PPA "is not
found in English," as Nelson Herle claimed.[32]

It should be noted that, out of all twelve of these texts, *not
one* uses an "aorist infinitive clause." Evidently, then, the
1950 NWT footnote (as well as the 1957 *Watchtower* and the
1969 *Kingdom Interlinear Translation*) was in error in citing
the "aorist infinitive clause" preceding the present tense
verb *eimi* as a reason for rendering *eimi* in a past tense.

One text which does have a past tense verb alongside a
present tense verb is Luke 2:48, where Mary says to Jesus,
". . . Here your father and I in mental distress [*odunōmenoi*]
have been looking [*ezētoumen*] for you" (NWT). This text,
however, is not at all parallel in grammatical form to John
8:58, nor to the genuine instances of the PPA. The verb
*odunōmenoi* is present passive participle, while *ezētoumen* is
imperfect active indicative. Since *ezētoumen*, the main verb, is
an imperfect (not a present) tense, it obviously cannot be a
PPA.[33] Rather, it is a vivid, idiomatic outburst (note that in
the context Mary's tone could reasonably be inferred to be
emotional). We could paraphrase her words as follows: "Your
father and I are going crazy looking for you!"

There is one text among these examples of the PPA which
appears at first in some sense to parallel John 8:58, namely,
2 Peter 3:4, which has the aorist verb *ekoimēthesan* ("fell
asleep") in the clause preceding the present tense verb *diamenei* ("are continuing"). However, this text does not help
the JWs' case at all. For one thing, as has already been

pointed out, they themselves render *diamenei* in the present tense. Also to be noticed is that *ekoimēthesan* is an aorist indicative, *not* an aorist infinitive. More important is the fact that the clause in which *ekoimēthesan* occurs is not the clause which makes *diamenei* a PPA. Rather, the critical clause is *ap' archēs ktiseōs* ("from creation's beginning"), since it tells us from which point "all things are continuing." Since this clause contains no verb at all, this text also is not parallel to John 8:58.

Two most critical observations, though, have yet to be made. The first comes from A. T. Robertson, who in his extensive discussion of the PPA points out in passing that in John 8:58 *"eimi* is really absolute,"* implying that for this reason it is not a true example of the PPA.[34] What Robertson means by "absolute" is that in John 8:58 *eimi* occurs as what is known as a predicate absolute, a construction in which a copulative verb is used without an object or complement.[35] A study of the relevant passages shows that none of them occur with predicate absolutes. Nor, apparently, *could* a predicate absolute be a PPA, since a predicate absolute does not express an action or ongoing event, nor even an ongoing specific condition, but rather simply existence. (Note that this does not mean that *eimi* cannot be used as a PPA in contexts where it is not a predicate absolute, as in John 14:9; 15:27; and 1 John 2:9). This point alone may not settle the matter, but it does point away from the identification of *eimi* in John 8:58 as a PPA.

Perhaps it should be noted that Nelson Herle has refused to admit that *eimi* in John 8:58 is a predicate absolute. Herle's discussions of this question in his letters and book suggest that he simply does not understand the terminology used by grammarians. Before examining what he says, it will be helpful to explain the terms involved. According to grammarians, the term *predicate* may be used in one of two ways: to refer to the verb itself, or to refer to a subject complement, adverbial expression, or modifier that follows a copulative (or "linking") verb. Thus, in the sentence, "Jack ran home," *ran* is a predicate in the first sense, while in the sentence, "Jack is at home," *at home* is a predicate in the second sense. A "predicate absolute" is simply a grammatical construction in which a linking verb is used without a predicate (in the second sense) expressed with it.

In a letter to Walter Martin, Herle took issue with Martin's statement (which was based on Robertson's assertion that *eimi* in John 8:58 is absolute) regarding *eimi* that "there is *no* predicate expressed with it."[36] Herle's response to this statement was to argue that *eimi* is indeed a predicate because it is a verb! His argument is as follows:

> However, let it be noted that Dr. Robertson at this point . . . is not commenting on the subject of parts of speech, but on that of *tense*. . . . His comment has nothing to do with the question "Does the word contain a predicate force or not?" His assigning the present tense to "Eimi" shows that it is a verb, since neither nouns nor verbal nouns have tense. To show that "Eimi" at Jo. 8:58 *does* express a predicate we need only refer to the lexicons. . . .[37]

What Herle has done here is to confuse the two meanings of the term *predicate* in grammar. When Martin (and other scholars) says that there is no predicate expressed with *eimi*, he is not denying that *eimi* is a verb (!), but simply observing that in John 8:58 *eimi* stands alone without any predicate expressed with it. Because *eimi* is a copulative verb (that is, one usually used to link subject and predicate), the absence of a predicate makes *eimi* a "predicate absolute."

This simple fact has been explained to Herle numerous times by Christians acquainted with grammar, yet he has not changed his position. In fact, in his book *The Trinity Doctrine*, he seems to understand exactly what a predicate absolute is, yet still refuses to admit that John 8:58 fits the description. After explaining that the occurrences of *egō eimi* in several texts (Isa. 41:4 LXX; 46:4 LXX; John 8:24, 28; 9:9) are predicate absolutes, he writes the following:

> A verb, such as ego is said to be a predicate absolute when it is used without an object. In the above citations, the expression "I am" itself does not have an object telling us what the subject is. "Ego" at John 8:58 is not used as "a predicate absolute" because it does not tell who the subject, Jesus, is; it is used, at this verse, to show that the Son of God was alive before Abraham. . . .[38]

What Herle is apparently trying to say here is that a verb is a predicate absolute only when it occurs without an "object" (that is, a predicate in the second sense) yet implies some sort of "object": for example, "I am" in John 9:9 means "I am the man" or the like. Such a qualification, however, is not given by any grammarian, and Herle does not attempt to document this definition at all. The fact is that any use of a copulative without a predicate expressed with it is a predicate absolute.

The second point has not before been specifically stated by grammarians with reference to John 8:58, but is based on the usual definition of the PPA as given by such grammarians as Robertson, Burton, Dana and Mantey, and others. As has already been noted, "an adverbial expression denoting duration and referring to past time" (as Burton put it[39]) usually accompanies the PPA—indeed, it *always* does in the genuine examples found in the New Testament. In each case, the relevant adverbial expression defines (whether in a vague, general manner or very specifically and exactly) the period and extent of the duration of the verb. These adverbial clauses make it explicit that the action or condition described by the present tense verb is a temporal one that began at some point in the past.

In Luke 13:7, for example, where the NWT reads, "Here it is three years that I have come looking . . . ," "it is three years" translates *tria etē aph' ou*, "three years from which." This clause clearly sets the action of the PPA verb *erchomai* ("I am coming") in the temporal past beginning roughly three years prior to the time of speaking. All of the other examples

of the PPA in the New Testament have similar clauses delim-
iting the time reference of the verb: "so many years" (*tosauta
etē,* Luke 15:29); "a long time" (*polun ēdē chronon,* John 5:6);
"so long a time" (*tosoutō chronō,* John 14:9); "from [the] beginning" (*ap' archēs,* John 15:27 [NWT, "from when I began"];
1 John 3:8); "from ancient times" (*ek geneōn archaiōn,* Acts
15:21); "all this while" (*palai,* 2 Cor. 12:19); "from infancy"
(*apo brephous,* 2 Tim. 3:15); "from creation's beginning" (*ap'
archēs ktiseōs,* 2 Peter 3:4); and "up to right now" (*heōs arti,*
1 John 2:9). All of these expressions refer to a period of time
beginning at some point (whether specified or not) in the
past and continuing up to the time of the speaker.

Not only is this not the case in John 8:58, the situation is
the precise opposite. There Jesus' existence is said to be
"*before* Abraham came into existence," so that the expression
does not refer to a period of time *beginning* at Abraham's
birth, but rather *ending* then. In other words, *prin Abraam
genesthai* does not point forward from Abraham's birth up to
the time of Jesus' speaking, but instead points *backward* from
Abraham's birth to the more distant past. To put it yet another way (since this point is critical and somewhat new), a
clause beginning with *prin* cannot specify "duration" up to
the present, since it refers to a period *prior* to the past event
specified in the clause. Had John wished to construct a clause
that did indicate duration, he could have said something like,
"since *(apo)* Abraham came into existence"; but as it stands,
*prin Abraam genesthai* does not fit the requirements of a clause
indicating the duration of a PPA verb.

Nelson Herle himself observes, "It can be seen from the
other examples of the 'present of past action still in progress'
from Luke through 1 John, that one fact is common to them
all; all these events had a beginning." He then states, without any evidence, "John 8:58 is no exception."[40] But as we
have seen, John 8:58 *is* an exception: there no beginning is
stated or implied, whereas in all the other texts, a beginning
was clearly implied for each.

Therefore, John 8:58 is not really an instance of the PPA. It is true, of course, that Jesus existed before Abraham, and that he continued to exist up until (and beyond) the day he spoke the words in John 8:58. It might be felt that in light of this observation *eimi* might properly be understood as a PPA, since Jesus both *was* and *is* existing from that time reference in which Jesus spoke. In this qualified sense it might be agreed that *eimi* in John 8:58 could be called a PPA; but if so, it would have to be with the understanding that it was a *different kind* of PPA. That is, it could be maintained that there are two kinds of PPA: those limited to temporal events, actions, and conditions, and those which refer to eternal states. However, in light of the fact that *eimi* is a predicate absolute, and because the text does not have the usual adverbial expression denoting the duration of the verb, the more accurate approach is simply to deny that John 8:58 is an actual instance of the PPA. In either case, the text will still have the same meaning—eternal preexistence.

How, then, should the text be translated? Most translations opt for "I am," while a few read "I have been" or the like; a very few render "I have been and still am" or the equivalent. The examples of 1 John 2:9 and 2 Peter 3:4 prove that the PPA need not be rendered in a past tense, but may if context requires. In John 8:58, however, the context demands the present tense rendering "I am," since translating any other way obscures the parallel with the other texts in John 8 in which Christ says *egō eimi* (8:12, 24, 28). The rendering "I have been," therefore, even though found in some translations, is not accurate.

That John 8:58 may be seen as a PPA yet also as an affirmation of eternal preexistence is demonstrated by Sanders and Mastin's commentary on John, which is apparently the only twentieth-century commentary which identifies John 8:58 as a PPA:

. . . the aorist *genesthai* "came into being," used of Abraham, is contrasted with the present *eimi,* which can express duration up to the present, "I have been <and still am>" as well as the simple present, "I am." Jesus claims that his mode of existence transcends time, like God's, and his *I am* is understood by the Jews as a claim to equality with God. . . .[41]

It is also worth noting that Sanders and Mastin agree that in John 8:58, along with other passages in John (6:20; 8:24, 28; 13:19; 18:5–8), "Jesus uses the words 'I am' *(Egō eimi)* without any predicate."[42]

The contrast between *genesthai* and *eimi* pointed out by Sanders and Mastin is the most critical factor in the interpretation of John 8:58, and it is to this contrast that our attention must now be turned.

## The Contrast Between Eternal and Created

It has long been recognized by commentators on the Gospel of John that in 8:58 a deliberate contrast is made between the created origin of Abraham and the eternal uncreated nature of Christ. This contrast is made by the use of *genesthai* for Abraham, but *eimi* for Christ. Thus, Augustine wrote, "Understand, that 'was made' refers to human formation; but 'am' to the Divine essence."[43]

Almost every commentary and scholarly work which discusses the interpretation of John 8:58 at any length notes this contrast, and most specifically state that the contrast is one of temporal origin versus eternal existence. A small sampling of these scholars would include such notables as Alford, Barclay, Barrett, Büchsel, Bultmann, Dodd, Lenski, Lindars, Robertson, Schnackenburg, Vincent, and Westcott.[44]

JWs are likely to object that the testimony of these numerous scholars may be discounted on the grounds that they are all trinitarian Christians. Such is not the case, however. Many nontrinitarian scholars who reject the Christ of the creeds and deny that Jesus is the eternal God, admit that *eimi* refers to the eternal preexistent past. How they go about maintaining such a position is instructive. Bultmann would see the "I am" as spoken by "the Revealer," who is *not* the historical person of Jesus.[45] Davey claims that John has misinterpreted the words of Jesus.[46] Davey's position is, in fact, the usual one among liberal theologians. Schnackenburg seems to affirm the preexistence and deity of Jesus, then turns about and states that Jesus was not claiming to be Yahweh, but only that in Jesus God had "come to them to fulfill his saving promises."[47] Since these scholars (Bultmann in particular) are renowned for their exegetical ability, it would seem likely that their exegesis is correct but their subsequent interpretation faulty due to their theological bias.

Moreover, this contrast has been recognized by both trinitarian and antitrinitarian scholars throughout the last 500 years or more. As has already been mentioned (in chapter 6), John Calvin debated persons in his day who interpreted the passage to mean that Jesus was eternally known by God in his foreknowledge. This view survived late into the nineteenth century, when it was effectively put to rest by the orthodox observation that the emphatic *egō* allowed for no other interpretation but that Jesus himself was the one who existed eternally. Thus, Godet, a famous nineteenth-century biblical scholar, wrote:

> "If," says Luthardt, "it follows from the apposition between *to be* and *to become*, in this saying, that the existence of Christ is eternal, it follows quite as clearly from the *egō* that this existence is personal." This, too, is proved by the comparison with Abraham. For there would have been a touch of charlatanism on the part of Jesus in suddenly substituting an impersonal principle for His Person, in His reply to the Jews, who were accusing Him of making Himself the contemporary of Abraham. If one of the two existences compared is personal, the other must be so too, otherwise this statement, marked as it is by the greatest solemnity, is not a serious one.[48]

Only by reading the Gospel of John as myth, as is seen in Bultmann's commentary and numerous other liberal works, do any modern scholars deny this interpretation.

As a matter of fact, JWs appear to be the first and only group of students of the Bible ever to argue that the contrast is anything less than that of created versus eternal being. This does not make their position *a priori* impossible, of course, but it does mean that the burden of proof is on them to come up with solid exegetical reasons for discarding an interpretation which has had such durability throughout the centuries.

What is it about this contrast between *genesthai* and *eimi* that has led to such a solid consensus throughout the centuries among biblical scholars that the words contrast created origin with uncreated eternal existence? By itself, of course, the word *eimi* does not connote eternal preexistence. However, placed alongside *genesthai* and referring to a time anterior to that indicated by *genesthai*, the word *eimi* (or its related forms), because it denotes simple existence and is a durative form of the verb *to be*, stands in sharp contrast to the aorist *genesthai* which speaks of "coming into being." It is this sharp contrast between *being* and *becoming* which makes it clear that in a text like John 8:58 *eimi* connotes eternality, not merely temporal priority.

Moreover, this is not the only text in John which draws this contrast between being and becoming. In his "Prologue" John contrasts the Word, which "was" (*ēn*, third person imperfect form of *eimi*) in the beginning, with his bringing into existence (*egeneto*, the third person singular indicative form of *genesthai*) of all things (John 1:1–3). As was explained in chapter 1, to say that the Word was continuing to exist at the beginning of created time is simply another way of saying that the Word was eternal. By going on to say that this uncreated Logos "became" (*egeneto*) flesh (1:14), John draws another contrast between the two natures of Christ. To put it in the classic terminology of orthodox incarnational theology, Christ was uncreated (*ēn*) with respect to his deity, but created (*egeneto*) with respect to his humanity.

It may be noted that in John 8:58, the contrast is not between two past tense verbs, one imperfect (*ēn*) and one aorist *(egeneto)*, as in John 1:1–3, but between a durative present tense verb *(eimi)* and an aorist past tense verb *(genesthai)*. The reason for the difference is not hard to see. In John 1:1–3 the event of "becoming" which is contrasted with the eternal existence of the Logos is the creation of the universe. To speak of something as already existing at the creation of the universe of space and time is simply one way of saying that it is timelessly eternal, since strictly speaking nothing can exist before the first instant of time. Thus, in John 1:1–2, the imperfect tense verb *ēn* connected with "in the beginning" clearly communicates the eternality of the Logos. In 8:58, on the other hand, the event of "becoming" with which Christ's eternal existence is contrasted is the birth of Abraham. Since Abraham's birth was preceded by thousands of years of human history, to have said no more than that Jesus existed before Abraham would not have communicated His eternality. Jesus therefore said more than that he preexisted Abraham. He chose the term that would most strongly contrast the created origin in time of Abraham with his own timeless eternality, the present tense verb *eimi*.

Thus, had Jesus wished to say what JWs understand him to have said—that he merely existed for a long time before Abraham—he could have said so by saying, "Before Abraham came into existence, I *was*," using the imperfect tense *ēmēn* instead of the present tense *eimi*. (This point was made by Chrysostom and Augustine, reaffirmed by such Reformers as Calvin, and is also a standard observation found in most exegetical commentaries on John and never, to this author's knowledge, disputed in such works.) Such a statement would have left open the question of whether or not Jesus had always existed, or whether (like the angels) he had existed from the earliest days of the universe's history. Or, had he wished to make it clear that (as the JWs believe) he had himself come into existence some time prior to Abraham, he could have said so by stating, "Before Abraham came into existence, I *came into existence*" (by using the first person aorist *egenomen* instead of *eimi*), or perhaps more simply, "I came into existence before Abraham." Having said neither of these things, but rather, having chosen terms which went beyond these other formulations to draw a contrast between the created and the uncreated, Jesus' words must be interpreted as a claim to eternality.

It may be wondered why, in making such a claim, Jesus should choose to contrast his eternality with the created origin of Abraham (rather than, say, the universe, as in 1:1–3). The immediate context of John 8 leaves no doubt as to the reason. Throughout the chapter Jesus and the Jews are discussing the nature of sonship to Abraham and sonship to God. Jesus is willing to grant that the Jews are sons of Abraham, although he is constrained to point out that they do not act like Abraham's sons (8:33–40). However, he emphatically denies that they are sons of God, and asserts that his actions prove that he honors his Father as a true Son would (8:41–51). This claim leads to a discussion of how Jesus, who promises that those who keep his word "will never see death," can claim to be greater than "our father Abraham who died" (8:52–55) and to have "seen Abraham" (8:56, 57). Jesus answered by contrasting his timeless eternality with the created, mortal temporality of Abraham (8:58).

# 8

## "I Am" as the Words of Jehovah

In the preceding chapter evidence was presented that in John 8:58 Jesus claimed to be eternal. This fact alone is enough to prove that Jesus' statement implies a claim to be Jehovah, the only true God. Even if John 8:58 could not be shown to reflect or allude to any Old Testament text at all, it would still stand as a prooftext for the absolute deity of Christ.

However, there are passages in the Old Testament which many biblical scholars believe to be significant for fully appreciating the words of Jesus in John 8:58. In this chapter we shall discuss the most important of these passages.

### John 8:58 and Psalm 90:2

That the contrast between *eimi* and *genesthai* in John 8:58 is intended to express a contrast between created origin and uncreated existence receives impressive confirmation by the parallel statement in the Septuagint translation of Psalm 90:2 (translating literally): "Before *(pro)* the mountains were brought into existence [*genēthēnai*] . . . from age to age, you are [*su ei*]." The parallels between this text and John 8:58 are remarkable.

The word *pro*, like *prin*, means "before," and some manuscripts of the Septuagint actually have *prin* instead of *pro*.[1]

117

The verb introduced by these prepositions in both cases is *ginomai:* in Psalm 90:2 *genēthēnai* is the aorist passive infinitive of *ginomai,* while in John 8:58 *genesthai* is the aorist active infinitive. The use of the active voice instead of the passive voice, of course, does not affect the parallel between the two texts in terms of the created-eternal contrast. These aorist infinitive phrases are then set in contrast to a present indicative main clause in each case: in Psalm 90:2 LXX it is *su ei,* while in John 8:58 it is *egō eimi.* These two clauses are identical in terms and meaning except for the fact that the former is second person while the latter is first person; and again, this difference does not affect the parallel in question.

Thus the tense-mood forms are identical, the syntactical relations between the two verbs in each passage are identical, and the verbs themselves used in each passage are identical. In other words, it is as if John (quoting Jesus' words in Greek) had taken the relevant words from Psalm 90:2 LXX, perhaps substituted *prin* for *pro,* replaced "the mountains" with "Abraham," and changed *su ei* from second person to first person and *genēthēnai* from passive to active. One could hardly ask for a more exact parallel, unless the passage itself were actually quoted. Since the parallel in question is fundamentally one of *tense* (since the issue is the significance in relation to time of the present tense of *eimi* in John 8:58), and since none of the differences between the two texts affect that parallel, it would seem safe to conclude that *eimi* has the same force in John 8:58 that *ei* has in Psalm 90:2 LXX. In Psalm 90:2, the Septuagint rendering *su ei* is clearly intended to assert the eternal preexistence of Yahweh in contrast to the created origin of the mountains. That this text, even in its Hebrew form, teaches the eternality of Yahweh has been frequently observed by the JWs themselves in their publications.[2] To be consistent, then, they would have to admit that John 8:58 just as clearly affirms the eternality of Jesus.

Once again, it must be understood that the position taken here is not original. A multitude of scholars have recognized the parallel between Psalm 90:2 LXX and John 8:58 and noted its significance as confirming that Jesus' words connote eternality. Among these should be mentioned Barnes, Barrett, Brown, Bultmann, Godet, Hengstenberg, Hoskyns, Lindars, Milligan and Moulton, Plummer, Robertson, Schnackenburg, and Winer.[3] Not one known biblical scholar has ever disputed the parallel or denied that it confirmed the traditional interpretation. Unless some important considerations have been overlooked, this exegetical conclusion would seem to be as well established as any could be.

One counterargument which JWs have offered in this matter is that the LXX rendering is not a literal translation of the Hebrew, which reads, "You are God," rather than the predicate absolute "You are."[4] Thus, it is claimed that the fact that the LXX has *su ei* instead of *su ei theos* rules out using Psalm 90:2 as a parallel to John 8:58.

It may be freely admitted that *su ei* is not a literal translation of the final clause of the Hebrew text of Psalm 90:2. However, to reason from that premise to the conclusion that Psalm 90:2 is irrelevant to John 8:58 requires an additional premise: namely, that for two passages to be parallel they must be identical, which is fallacious. Indeed, the New Testament frequently and freely *quotes* from the LXX in places where it is even less of a literal translation of the Hebrew than in Psalm 90:2, and in other places quotes the Old Testament in a form that does not match exactly either the Hebrew or the LXX texts (compare, for example, Ps. 8:5 with Heb. 2:7; Ps. 68:18 with Eph. 4:8).[5] More important, it is not even being claimed that John 8:58 quotes Psalm 90:2; all that is being claimed is that the two texts are parallel in their use of a contrast between forms of *eimi* and *genesthai* to connote a contrast between temporal and eternal existence. This would be so, even if Psalm 90:2 LXX were not in the Bible at all, but was a piece of extrabiblical Greek (although the fact that it is LXX Greek strengthens the case). It is the grammatical and syntactical parallels between the two texts that matter in this case—nothing else.

That the reasoning of the JWs is without substance can be further seen in the fact that the difference between the Hebrew "You are God" and the Greek "You are" is quite slight. By using the predicate complement "God," the Hebrew does emphasize the fact that Yahweh has not only existed eternally, but has existed eternally *as God*. But since the LXX emphasizes Yahweh's unchangeableness while acknowledging elsewhere that Yahweh is God, it is evident that the LXX rendering in the end means the same thing as the Hebrew original.

### John 8:58 and "I Am" in Isaiah

Among biblical scholars a growing consensus has formed behind the opinion that John 8:58 deliberately echoes Yahweh's "I am" statements in Isaiah 40–55. The NWT obscures the parallels in Isaiah by rendering them "I am the same One" or "I am the same"; but the Hebrew in each case reads simply ANI HU (literally, "I [am] he"), which the LXX renders as *egō eimi* (Isa. 41:4; 43:10; 46:4; 52:6; compare with Deut. 32:39). The words ANI HU, unlike EHYEH in Exodus 3:14 (to be discussed further in this chapter), are not used in Isaiah as a title. There is evidence, moreover, to show that in the Judaism of Jesus' day these words were sometimes used as substitutes for the divine name Yahweh itself, in particular at the Feast of Tabernacles, which from John 7:2 was apparently the occasion of Christ's "I am" sayings in John 8. This suggests that the reason for the anger of the Jews at Jesus' absolute use of the expression *egō eimi* was that on that occasion his language was instantly recognizable as that of Yahweh.

Once again, a large number of biblical scholars have defended this conclusion, and very few deny it.[6] The sole objection offered by the JWs is that David said ANI HU in 1 Chronicles 21:17,[7] an objection which fails to note that David's use of the phrase is completely nontheological. The JWs might just as well argue that Jesus' use of *egō eimi* in John

8:58 means nothing more than "It is I," since this is its meaning on the lips of the blind man in John 9:9. The only biblical scholar known to this author who disputes the connection between John and Isaiah is Joseph Crehan, who argues for a close connection with Exodus 3:14 instead.[8]

Considerations such as these have led most scholars to conclude that the closest Old Testament antecedent to John 8:58 is to be found in the Isaianic "I am" sayings. If this is correct, the conclusion cannot be avoided that Jesus was claiming to be Yahweh. Notable in this light is Isaiah 45:18, where God says, "I am Yahweh" (Hebrew, ANI HU YHWH), and the LXX translates simply by the predicate absolute *egō eimi*. The LXX is also relevant in its rendering of Exodus 3:14, to which we now turn.

### John 8:58 and Exodus 3:14

In popular evangelical apologetics, it has been commonplace for Christians to argue for the deity of Christ from John 8:58 by simply connecting that text with Exodus 3:14, where, in most translations, Yahweh tells Moses that his name is "I Am." It is this connection with Exodus 3:14, above anything else, that JWs wish to avoid in their interpretation of John 8:58, since they are committed to denying that Jesus is Jehovah. Indeed, it appears most probable that the rendering "I have been" in the NWT was chosen because it avoids any association of John 8:58 with Exodus 3:14. The JWs have therefore given special attention to denying any connection between the two texts.[9]

Nevertheless, it is not very important whether such a connection can be established. Even if Exodus 3:14 were not in the Bible at all, John 8:58 would stand on its own as an assertion of the eternality of Christ, as the foregoing discussion has sought to demonstrate (perhaps to the extent of overkill!). If Christ is eternal and uncreated, then he is Yahweh, for only Yahweh is eternal and uncreated. Therefore, it is not at all necessary for the Christian to prove any connection at all between John 8:58 and Exodus 3:14 in order to use John 8:58 as a prooftext for the deity of Christ. For instance, the early church fathers did not, as a rule, appeal to Exodus 3:14 to explain John 8:58, but rather emphasized the contrast between *genesthai* and *eimi* as indicating eternality. This does not mean that the early church did not notice the connection, or that the connection is invalid; but it does suggest that less emphasis should be placed on Exodus 3:14 in interpreting John 8:58 than is usually the case in evangelical defenses of the deity of Christ.

On the other hand, of course, it is absolutely necessary for the JW to discount any such connection. Even if the JWs are correct in denying the connection, though, their case cannot be established without also demonstrating that John 8:58 need not be interpreted as a claim to eternality on the part of Christ.

JWs have offered the following arguments against taking John 8:58 as a claim by Jesus to be the "I Am" of Exodus 3:14 and therefore Yahweh:

1. Jesus was speaking of his preexistence, not his identity; the question was *when* he was, not *who* he was.
2. In John 8:58 *egō eimi* is not a title, as is EHYEH in Exodus 3:14.
3. The Septuagint rendering of EHYEH (usually translated "I Am" in English translations) is not *egō eimi*, but *ho ōn*.
4. The meaning of the Hebrew EHYEH is not "I am," but "I will be" or "I shall prove to be."
5. Several reputable biblical scholars deny any connection between John 8:58 and Exodus 3:14.

An examination of each of these arguments will show that none of them decisively disproves that Jesus was claiming to be the One who spoke to Moses in Exodus 3:14.

Nelson Herle seems to have introduced to JWs the argument that in John 8:58 Jesus "only disclosed *when* he was alive, sometime before Abraham, not who he was,"[10] although one commentator in the nineteenth century, Olshausen, did use a similar argument.[11] (Olshausen, though, agreed that Jesus was claiming to be the eternal, uncreated God; he simply denied that Exodus 3:14 was relevant to the exegesis of the text.) The argument has recently been repeated in Watchtower literature.[12] A careful study of the context, however, shows that Jesus was in fact discussing his identity. It has already been noted at the end of the last chapter that the subject at hand was Jesus' extraordinary claim to a unique relationship with God as his Son. The entire passage consists of a series of discussions of the identity of Jesus. Indeed, so much is this the case that C. K. Barrett, in his commentary on John, entitled John 8:12–59 "Who Is Jesus?"[13]

The passage begins with an emphatic statement by Jesus about his identity (v. 12); notably, the statement begins with the words *egō eimi* ("I am the light of the world"). Then follows a discussion of the validity of this statement, ending with Christ's assertion, "YOU know neither me nor my Father" (v. 19)—that is, they do not know the true identity of Jesus. In the next segment, Jesus makes some strong statements, ending with the warning (translating literally), "Unless you believe that *I am* [italics added], you will die in your sins" (v. 24). Whatever else may be the meaning of the words "I am" *(egō eimi)* here, the statement clearly means that the Jews will suffer condemnation unless they acknowledge Jesus' true identity. The Jews' response, naturally, is to ask, "Who are you?" (v. 25). Jesus' response is to note that he has been telling them all along, but that they will only know "that *I am*" after his death (vv. 26–30). Then follows the interchange concerning the Jews as sons of Abraham and Jesus as the Son of God, ending with the Jews repeating the question, "Who do you claim to be?" (v. 53). Jesus' response is that he was the one in whom Abraham rejoiced, a claim which the Jews found incredible in light of his obvious youth (vv. 54–57). Their confusion was apparently along these lines: Who is this man, who, while still in the prime of life, claims to have been Abraham's contemporary?

Thus, Jesus' response to the Jews' question did not deal merely with his age to the exclusion of his identity. Jesus was giving both a direct answer to their immediate question ("How can you have seen Abraham?") and an indirect answer to their underlying concern made explicit twice earlier ("Just who do you think you are?"). Rather than force an "either/or" (*either* Jesus was talking about his age *or* about his identity) on the text, the context would indicate that we should recognize Jesus' statement as "both/and" (Jesus was saying something about his preexistence and his identity).

A second common argument used by the Witnesses is that *egō eimi* in John 8:58 is not a title, as is EHYEH in Exodus 3:14.[14] Many Christian writers have said that in John 8:58 Jesus was laying hold of the divine title "I Am,"[15] and this is a point which JWs obviously cannot accept. On this matter some balance needs to be found. Jesus certainly does not say, in so many words, "I am the 'I Am,'" nor does he quote Exodus 3:14 in its entirety and apply it to himself. The words *egō eimi* in John 8:58 do not function as a title of Christ, but are a statement of his eternality (and, implicitly, his deity). Nevertheless, the fact that we cannot speak of "I am" in this text as, strictly speaking, a "title," does not mean that John 8:58 does not in any way allude to Exodus 3:14. It may be that John intends Jesus' words to be understood not only as a claim to eternality, but also as an echo of Yahweh's words in Exodus 3:14.

Perhaps the most common objection given by JWs to connecting John 8:58 with Exodus 3:14 is that the LXX rendering of EHYEH is not *egō eimi* ("I am") but *ho ōn* ("the Being," or more idiomatically, "the One who is").[16] This is not quite telling the whole truth, however. What the text actually says in the LXX is as follows (translating literally):

> And God said to Moses,
> "I am [*egō eimi*] the One who is [*ho ōn*]";
> and He said,
> "Thus you shall say to the sons of Israel,
> 'The One who is [*ho ōn*] has sent me to you.'"

The statement *egō eimi ho ōn* here renders the Hebrew EHYEH ASHER EHYEH, which is usually translated into English as "I am who I am." Thus, the LXX has rendered the word EHYEH in two different ways, by both *egō eimi* and *ho ōn*. In its first occurrence, EHYEH is not used as a title, and the Septuagint renders it *egō eimi*; when it is used as a title ("I am EHYEH," "EHYEH has sent me to you"), the LXX renders it as *ho ōn*. It may very well be, then, that in John 8:58 the apostle John chooses the words *egō eimi* to translate Jesus' words as an allusion to Exodus 3:14 without construing Jesus' words as a title.

A fourth objection that has been raised is that "I am" (the literal rendering of *egō eimi*) is not a literal translation of EHYEH, which most Hebraists now recognize to mean literally "I will be," with the connotation of "I shall prove to be."[17] Although many evangelical scholars have argued that "I am" is correct, there would appear to be solid reasons for accepting the rendering "I will be" or "I will become."[18] This would make the meaning of EHYEH ASHER EHYEH to be "I will be what I will be," or some such equivalent. Because this is one of the few points on which the JWs have substantial evidence for their argument, many of them have given this one point a great deal of attention, even to the exclusion of other relevant points.[19]

If "I am what I am" is interpreted as a statement of self-existence, this would indeed seem not to be the point which Yahweh was seeking to make. That is, he was not trying to say, "I am the self-existent one," as many have interpreted Exodus 3:14. But this thought, while evidently not the point of EHYEH ASHER EHYEH, is not *foreign* to that expression.

There is no sound reason, to begin with, to accept the modern liberal contention that the concept of self-existence was
foreign to the "Hebrew mind" and was introduced later by
the Greeks.[20] Nor are the expressions "I am what I am" and
"I will be what I will be" all that dissimilar in meaning. Both
can suggest self-determination (or *sovereignty,* as evangelical
theologians would say), the fact that God will be whatever he
chooses to be, and that he cannot be circumscribed or
pigeonholed in the way that the gods of the nations were.
That this was Yahweh's meaning is suggested by the context,
in which Moses asked God by what name he should be
known. As Walther Zimmerli has stated:

> In this figure of speech resounds the sovereign freedom of
> Yahweh, who, even at the moment he reveals his name, re-
> fuses simply to put himself at the disposal of humanity to
> comprehend him . . . In the only passage where the Old
> Testament itself attempts to provide an explanation of the
> name "Yahweh" it refuses to explain the name in a way that
> would confine it within the cage of a definition.[21]

Charles Gianotti objects to this interpretation of Exodus
3:14 on the grounds that the text "gives no hint that Moses
asked amiss" and that "I AM" does seem to be used as a
name in that passage.[22] However, it is not necessary for
God's reply to be a rebuke for Zimmerli's position to be
correct. It may be simply that God is saying that his "name,"
as an expression of his character (as Gianotti says himself[23]),
cannot completely define or pigeonhole God in the way that
names of pagan deities were understood to do. The name
EHYEH does mean something (God's answer is not a facile "I
have no name" or a rude "None of your business"!)—but
rather means (at least in part) that God is sovereign and self-
determinative.

Indeed, Yahweh's response suggests that he does not have
a "name" in the same way that the pagan gods had names,
for he was not one god among many (a situation which

would call for distinctive names), but the only real God. This truth is affirmed in the Christian practice of referring to the God of the Bible simply as "God," implying that there really is no other being deserving of that title. Jehovah's Witnesses frequently object to this practice, arguing that it is not sufficient to call Yahweh "God," since the unbelieving nations worship many gods. Instead, they insist, true believers ought to call God by his "personal name," which they say is "Jehovah." The most important objection to this argument (many could be given) is that it ignores the practice of the Greek New Testament, which refers to the Supreme Being over and over again simply as "God," and never uses the appellative "Jehovah" or "Yahweh." Recognizing the damaging nature of this testimony, the Jehovah's Witnesses have inserted the name "Jehovah" in the New Testament portion of the NWT over 200 times in place of "Lord" or occasionally "God," sometimes as a result obscuring testimonies to the deity of Christ. This practice has been thoroughly analyzed and refuted elsewhere.[24] In light of the apparent meaning of the name "Yahweh" and the expression EHYEH ASHER EHYEH, it would seem that the Old Testament itself laid the foundation for the eventual obsolescence of the name "Yahweh" in Christian piety, as validated by the New Testament.

The name EHYEH, then, apparently connotes sovereignty, absolute independence, and self-determination. But to say that God is absolutely sovereign in this manner is not very far at all from asserting his self-existence! Indeed, orthodox theologians have always argued (biblically and philosophically) that God could not be truly independent from his creation and absolutely sovereign over it unless he were himself self-existent and eternal. JWs, for all their heterodox teachings, do agree that Jehovah is self-existent and eternal, so it would seem doubtful that they would disagree with this reasoning. Ironically, then, it would appear that Exodus 3:14 does contain at the very least a hint of Yahweh's self-existence and eternality, so that the wording "I am what I am" is not wrong after all. Consequently, this argument fails to disprove any connection between Exodus 3:14 and John 8:58.

The foregoing reasoning has assumed what the JWs here seem to take for granted, that an allusion to Exodus 3:14 must be based on the *Hebrew* text. Yet there is no reason to make such an assumption. John may have chosen to use the LXX rendering of EHYEH in its first occurrence in Exodus 3:14 as *egō eimi* to report Jesus' words to the Jews in John 8:58.

The fifth and final type of argument used by the JWs to discount any connection between John 8:58 and Exodus 3:14 is an appeal to biblical scholars who also deny the connection.[25] The impression often given is that modern scholars as a whole have rejected the allusion. The fact is, however, that most biblical scholars still see some relationship between the two texts. Among these are such scholars as Davey, Morris, Richardson, Sanders, Schnackenburg, Strachan, and Tasker,[26] some of whom (for example, Davey, Schnackenburg, Strachan) are not orthodox Christians. Some do deny the allusion, of course, but not many: Barrett,[27] Bultmann,[28] and Lindars[29] are the main modern representatives of this denial among commentators on the Gospel of John, along with the nineteenth-century scholar Olshausen, discussed earlier in this chapter. None of these scholars, as has already been noted, dispute that *eimi* in John 8:58 connotes eternality (although Bultmann does deny the deity of Jesus Christ).

The *reasons* that these scholars have for rejecting the allusion are what is important, not the mere fact that they reject it. In checking to see what reasons they give, it turns out that Barrett refers us to Lindars ("Lindars is right in saying . . ."), while Lindars repeats an argument made by Bultmann. Bultmann argues that the connection between the two texts "rests on the belief that *egō eimi* renders one of the mysterious Jewish formulas" used as substitutes for the divine name.[30] Some scholars (e.g., Odeberg, cited by Bultmann) have constructed the argument for the allusion in such a way, and if that were Jesus' (or John's) intention we would normally expect to find something like "I am the 'I am'" instead of the simple "I am." However, it is not necessary for Odeberg and others to be right about the divine name substitutes in order for John 8:58 to allude to Exodus 3:14. Bultmann's argument is therefore forced and overly rigid, since it is based on an invalid "either/or": *either* John 8:58 uses *egō eimi* from Exodus 3:14 as a "formula" substitute for the divine name, or it does not allude to Exodus 3:14 at all. This argument, in fact, is simply a more sophisticated form of the Witnesses' second argument, that John 8:58 cannot be alluding to Exodus 3:14 because it does not use *egō eimi* as a title.

## An Assertion of Deity

As has already been said, it is not necessary to prove a connection between John 8:58 and Exodus 3:14 to demonstrate that Jesus was making a claim to deity in John 8:58. The claim to eternality necessarily presupposes a claim to deity from within a Hebrew, theistic world view. Yet, it is still true that Jesus stops short of saying, in just so many words, "I am Yahweh," or "I am God." In keeping with his repeated self-declared purpose to reveal the Father and wait for the Father to vindicate and reveal his Son, Jesus studiously avoided calling himself "Yahweh" or "God." In making statements like that in John 8:58, though, his true identity was indirectly revealed to those who were willing to receive it. To those who were present, his statements were simply blasphemous, as their attempt to stone him indicates (8:59; cf. 10:33; Mark 2:7). Thus, William Temple commented on this text:

> There is no doubt now about the assertion of an eternal personality; there can be hardly any doubt about the claim to Deity. Yet it is made by allusion and implication. The words *I AM* need not of necessity mean more than an assertion of existence; they need not be the Divine Name revealed to Moses at the Bush (*Exodus* iii, 14). It still cannot be said that He has explicitly affirmed His Deity. That He will never do— as we shall find again at x, 30–36; the apprehension of that

truth must come through the response of men's souls. But he does lead us to the very verge of it. And if it is not true His language is the grossest blasphemy.[31]

It is ironic to find JWs quoting selectively from this passage in Temple's commentary in such a way as to try to construe him to deny that Jesus was claiming to be Yahweh.[32] When Temple says that "I am" need not "mean more than an assertion of existence," he obviously means *eternal* existence, as the first sentence quoted above demonstrates; but by omitting that sentence, the JWs try to make Temple say that Jesus was merely claiming to exist some time before Abraham. In a similar vein, Temple's statement that Jesus "will never" explicitly affirm his deity is construed to mean that Jesus did not at all claim to be Yahweh. Besides ignoring the qualifying adverb "explicitly," this misreading ignores the last half of that sentence and the subsequent two sentences (which the JWs typically omit when quoting Temple). As it stands, Temple's comments quite accurately summarize the point of John 8:58, and are clear in recognizing this text as one of the strongest prooftexts for the deity of Christ from the lips of the Lord himself.

# Conclusion

In this book we have examined two key texts that figure prominently in most discussions between evangelical Christians and JWs about the person of Jesus Christ. The first of these, John 1:1, is a powerful prooftext not only for the deity of Christ, but also for the trinitarian distinction between the Father and the Son as two persons in the one true God. The second text, John 8:58, is a claim by Jesus Christ to be eternal and therefore implicitly to be Jehovah.

Faced with the evidence for the interpretation of these two texts presented here, JWs may do one of the following things. *First,* they may refuse to listen. This reaction is common, because the JWs are constantly told not to listen to outsiders. It does not say much for their "truth," however, that it is so fragile it cannot stand up under close scrutiny.

*Second,* some JWs may answer this evidence by fleeing to other biblical texts that supposedly disprove the deity of Christ. This tactic falsely assumes that those other prooftexts clearly and unmistakably support their position, which they do not. It also implies that the Bible contradicts itself, by suggesting that passages like John 1:1 and 8:58 really do teach that Jesus is God, but other texts say differently. In their better moments, JWs agree that this is not so; they ought, then, to deal directly with John 1:1 and 8:58, and not run to other verses for shelter.

*Third,* many JWs will change the subject completely to a topic in which they have greater confidence that they are right. Many times, after Christians have presented JWs with irrefutable evidence that Jesus is Jehovah, JWs will say that although they cannot answer these arguments, they know they have "the truth" because JWs don't participate in wars or politics, or don't celebrate Christmas (these are by far the most common fall-back topics). It turns out that most JWs joined because of what the JWs *don't* do, not because of what they do or what they believe. Nevertheless, an exercise such as this book is necessary because of the many JWs who find security in their beliefs because of the alleged "biblical scholarship" of the Society in its treatment of John 1:1 and 8:58 and other texts.

*Fourth,* a few JWs will nitpick at minor points of the arguments presented in this book and ignore or sideswipe the major issues. A fifteen-page earlier draft of the section on John 8:58 was presented in 1984 to four JWs (including Nelson Herle) who claimed to be able to read Greek, and they were invited to tear apart its arguments. None of these JWs offered substantial criticisms of the major points of the paper, although they did continue to speak knowledgeably about "the Greek" of John 8:58 and other texts when talking to others. Instead, these JW "apologists" picked away at minor side issues (such as the precise translation of Exodus 3:14) and ignored the heart of what I was saying.

*Fifth,* some JWs will, by God's grace, realize that they have been following error and call on Jesus as Jehovah, their Lord and God (John 20:28; Acts 7:59–60; Rom. 10:9–13; 1 Cor. 1:2; and so forth). If you are a Jehovah's Witness, I urge you to consider the possibility that God the Father may be seeking to draw you to Jesus as your God (John 6:44). If you are a Christian who knows God as Father, Son, and Holy Spirit, I urge you to pray for the JWs you know, that many will hear the voice of the Son of God and follow him as their divine Shepherd.

# Appendix A
## John 20:28

That Jesus is called "my God" *(ho theos mou)* by Thomas in John 20:28 is generally not disputed by JWs. Some JWs have tried to counter the force of the definite article here by citing Moule:

> . . . it is to be noted that a substantive in the Nominative case used in a vocative sense and followed by a possessive could not be anarthrous (see Hoskyns and Davey, *Commentary, in loc.*); the article before *theos* may, therefore, not be significant.[1]

While Moule is quite correct in noting that the article is grammatically required in this instance, the text is still a powerful statement that Jesus is God, since it is a believer in the true God who calls Jesus "my God." The fact is that the use of the possessive "my" makes "God" definite, with or without the article, since now "God" is used to refer to a specific God—that is, Thomas's God.

The JW book *Aid to Bible Understanding* quotes with approval the *Imperial Bible Dictionary* when it says the following:

> The Hebrew may say *the* Elohim, the true God, in opposition to all false gods; but he never says *the* Jehovah, for Jehovah is the name of the true God only. He says again and again *my* God . . . but never *my* Jehovah, for when he says *my God,* he means Jehovah.[2]

Since Thomas was a Hebrew and a believer, for him to call Jesus "my God," then, was equivalent to calling him Jehovah. This conclusion is also supported by the fact that in Psalm 35:23 the expression "my God and my Lord" is used of Jehovah.

133

An interesting parallel to John 20:28 is Revelation 4:11, "You are worthy, our Lord and God" *(ho kurios kai ho theos hēmōn)*, which the NWT translates, "You are worthy, Jehovah, even our God. . . ." The only differences between this text and John 8:58 are (1) the possessive pronoun is singular in John ("my") and plural in Revelation ("our"); and (2) the pronoun is not repeated in Revelation, while it is repeated in John. Since in both cases the two nouns refer to one person, the fact that in Revelation 4:11 *hēmōn* ("our") appears only once does not alter the parallel. What makes this parallel especially striking is that JWs agree with conservative Christians that the same man, John the apostle, was the author of both the Gospel of John and the Book of Revelation. In this light, it seems likely that John 20:28 should be interpreted in a manner similar to Revelation 4:11.

# Appendix B

*How Scholars Have Translated John 1:1*

At the end of chapter 4 the question was raised as to how best to translate the last clause of John 1:1. It was pointed out that "the Word was God" was acceptable as long as this was not misinterpreted to mean that the Word was the same person as God the Father. The translations "the Word was Deity," "the Word was deity," and "the Word was divine" are all also acceptable, as long as they are understood to mean that the Word was *theos* in the same sense as *ton theon* while distinguished as personally distinct from *ton theon*. The translation "the Word was a god" was found inadequate because in English it conveys the idea that the Word was a second divine being (contradicting biblical monotheism) of a lesser, inferior divinity (contradicting John's use of *theos*).

It may be wondered if this perspective reflects the manner in which biblical scholars have actually translated John 1:1 in the published translations of the New Testament. A favorite tactic of JWs in arguing for the acceptability of their translation's rendering "the Word was a god" is to cite other translations which do not adopt the traditional rendering "the Word was God." Any rendering which deviates from this traditional wording is seized on as proof that the NWT rendering is supported by unbiased biblical scholarship after all.

Nothing could be further from the truth. The vast majority of translations of the New Testament either follow the traditional rendering or adopt wordings such as "the Word was divine," which, as we have already seen, supports the trinitarian interpretation, not the JW understanding of John 1:1. While it may be freely admitted that there are a few translations which do not interpret John 1:1 in a manner consistent with trinitarianism, these are no embarrassment to the orthodox Christian, as shall be explained shortly.

Below we present an analysis of the nontraditional renderings of John 1:1 cited by JWs in defense of their translation.[1] It should be kept in mind that for every one translation listed below, there are at least four or five currently circulating English translations which follow the traditional rendering or some equivalent. Also, nearly every translation done by a committee has translated John 1:1 in a manner consistent with the trinitarian interpretation; the only exception known to this writer is the NWT committee. For simplicity's sake, the rendering of *theos* alone is given in the far left column, as this is the sole matter of controversy.

Table 2  **Nontraditional Translations of John 1:1**

| John 1:1c *(theos)* | Translations | Comments |
| --- | --- | --- |
| *deity* | Simple English Bible | As already explained, this translation supports the orthodox view, not the JW one. |
| *divine* | Moffatt; Goodspeed; Schonfield | Same as above. |
| *a God* | Abner Kneeland; Robert Young; James L. Tomanec | This rendering is probably an attempt to reflect the lack of a definite article in the Greek; thus, Young writes, "more lit. 'and a God' (i.e. a Divine Being) was the Word."[2] Note that God is called "a God" in Luke 20:38. Kneeland and Tomanec are not known scholars. |
| *god* | C. C. Torrey | Translating "god" rather than "a god" may have been an attempt to avoid implying polytheism while reflecting the subtle difference between *ton theon* and *theos*. |

| John 1:1c *(theos)* | Translations | Comments |
|---|---|---|
| *a god* | New Testament in an Improved Edition; Emphatic Diaglott (interlinear); Johannes Greber; John S. Thompson; Jurgen Becker; Siegfried Schulz | The "Improved Edition" was unitarian; the Diaglott was by Benjamin Wilson, who denied Christ's deity; Johannes Greber was a spiritist who translated based on messages from the spirit world. (The JWs have stopped citing Greber.) Most of these works are not by scholars.[3] |
| *deistic; of divine being; of divine weightiness; God of a sort; godlike sort* | A. L. Totten; Stage; Menge; Pfaefflin; Thimme; Schneider | These renderings are paraphrases, not translations. The word *theos* never means any of these things, and never in Greek literature will one find *theos* so rendered. Nor do these paraphrases accurately express the meaning of the clause as a whole. |
| *What God was, the Word was; the Word was with God and shared his nature* | New English Bible; Translator's New Testament | These renderings are also paraphrases. However, they do accurately express the meaning of the clause as a whole; and they express the orthodox reading of the text, not the JW view. |

# Appendix C
## How Scholars Have Translated John 8:58

In Part 2 of this book the translation "I am" of *egō eimi* in John 8:58 was favored as the best rendering over such renderings as "I have been" and "I was." It was pointed out in chapter 7 that the rendering "I am," besides being the most literal, is the only rendering which preserves the parallel in the near context with the previous *egō eimi* statements (8:12, 24, 28), as well as the other such statements throughout John. The "I am" rendering also preserved the parallels with Exodus 3:14 (whether this parallel is partial or exact) and the "I am" statements in Isaiah 40–48. The translations "I have been," "I was," "I have been and still am," though not strictly speaking grammatically incorrect, are also misleading in that they generally imply to the English reader that Jesus was only claiming to have existed prior to Abraham, whereas his claim was actually to be eternal in contrast to Abraham as temporal.

In an attempt to legitimize their interpretation of John 8:58, the JWs often cite a long list of translations which render John 8:58 in a manner similar to the NWT. It must be freely admitted that a fairly long list of such translations can be compiled. For instance, Nelson Herle has put together a list of some 21 translations that avoid the simple "I am."[1] What Herle fails to note is that there are some sixty other translations which he himself cites elsewhere in his book which do not support his view of John 8:58. Moreover, not one of these twenty-one translations includes any kind of commentary or footnote supporting the JW *interpretation* of John 8:58, according to

139

which Jesus was only claiming to have been created before Abraham.

Still, it is worth noting some facts about the twenty-one translations listed by Nelson Herle. A few of them are by noted biblical scholars (Moffatt, Goodspeed, Williams), and one of them is a popular evangelical translation which in a marginal note in its earlier editions gave "I have been" as a possible alternate rendering (the New American Standard Bible). Almost all of the rest of them, however, are by obscure or controversial figures whose scholarship is open to question. This is especially true of Stage, Pfaefflin, Sharpe, Lewis, Noyes, and Schonfield. Hugh Schonfield is the Jewish scholar who wrote *The Passover Plot*, in which he argued that Jesus faked death on the cross to fake a resurrection.

Several more are based on translations from the Greek into another language. For example, Herle lists Lamsa, who was translating into English the Aramaic translation of the Greek New Testament; he also lists Salkinson and Ginsburg's translation of the New Testament into Hebrew. The problem with such citations is that a translation of a translation is generally not as reliable as a translation based on the original language.

In conclusion, the scholarly representation for the "I have been" translation is not nearly as impressive as the JWs would like to claim. In their better moments JWs agree that scholarly opinion is true only when it agrees with the facts. As we have seen, the facts support neither the "I have been" translation of John 8:58 nor the JW interpretation of that text as being only a claim to temporal preexistence on the part of Christ.

# Appendix D
## Letter to The Watchtower Bible and Tract Society

On the following page is reproduced the author's letter to the Watchtower Bible and Tract Society, inviting them to request a prepublication manuscript of this book and write a rebuttal to the book. Similar letters were sent to Nelson Herle, Nicholas Kip, and other Jehovah's Witnesses. None of these letters was even acknowledged.

**CRI**✝ CHRISTIAN RESEARCH INSTITUTE

Post Office Box 500
San Juan Capistrano CA 92693-0500
714/855-9926

October 22, 1987

Watch Tower Bible and Tract Society
25 Columbia Heights
Brooklyn, NY 11201

Dear Sirs:

I realize that you receive a great deal of mail. Still, I hope that whoever reads this letter first will see to it that it is routed to the proper person. I would be very pleased if it were routed to Mr. Franz or another member of the Governing Body, but I realize that may not be possible.

No doubt you are already well aware of our organization and its publications. I have recently completed a manuscript for a book entitled Jehovah's Witnesses, Jesus Christ, and the Gospel of John, to be published by an evangelical publishing house. This book, which in manuscript form is approximately 180 pages, deals almost exclusively with examining carefully the translation and interpretation of John 1:1 and John 8:58 in the publications of the Watch Tower.

It is my desire to be as fair to your organization as possible. In a recent article in Awake! it was stated that the Watch Tower publications present all of the arguments for and against a position and then leave it to the reader to decide, while trinitarian publications, it was suggested, present a one-sided view of the truth. I want your point of view to be fully heard by the readers of my book, so they can decide for themselves.

Therefore, I would like to invite any Jehovah's Witness who is willing and able to write a response or rebuttal to my book. The response, which may be up to about 10,000 words in length (roughly 30-40 pages), will be included in the book as an appendix. The rebuttal will be edited only for clarity and style, and its author will be given a chance to examine the edited version for approval before it is published. The person who writes the rebuttal may remain anonymous, although his name will be given if you wish.

If you wish to have such a rebuttal representing your viewpoint published in the book, I need to receive a letter from you by January 2, 1988, stating your intention to submit a response. The response itself must be sent to me by June 1, 1988. A copy of the table of contents is enclosed; I will send the entire manuscript to you when I receive your letter.

I hope to hear from you soon.

Sincerely in Christ,

Robert M. Bowman, Jr.
Associate Editor
Christian Research Institute

# Notes

## Introduction

1. Philip B. Harner, "Qualitative Anarthrous Predicate Nouns: Mark 15:39 and John 1:1," *Journal of Biblical Literature* 92, 1 (March 1973):75–87.

2. Nelson Herle, *The Trinity Doctrine Examined in the Light of History and the Bible* (unpublished manuscript, 1st ed. 1983; 2nd ed. 1987).

3. A good introduction to the inspiration, text, and canon of the Bible is Norman L. Geisler and William E. Nix, *A General Introduction to the Bible*, rev. ed. (Chicago: Moody Press, 1986). Two books on biblical inerrancy are R. C. Sproul, *Explaining Inerrancy: A Commentary*, International Council on Biblical Inerrancy (ICBI) Foundation Series No. 2 (Oakland, CA: ICBI, 1980), a commentary on the ICBI Chicago Statement on Biblical Inerrancy; and Norman L. Geisler (ed.), *Inerrancy* (Grand Rapids: Zondervan Publishing Company, 1980). A standard textbook on logic is Irving M. Copi, *Introduction to Logic*, 6th ed. (New York: Macmillan Publishing Co., 1982); unfortunately, at two points Copi accuses the Bible (quite erroneously) of containing logical fallacies. Two introductory books on biblical interpretation are R. C. Sproul, *Knowing Scripture* (Downers Grove, IL: InterVarsity Press, 1977), a positive treatment, and James Sire, *Scripture Twisting* (Downers Grove, IL: InterVarsity Press, 1980), on how *not* to interpret the Bible. On the use of biblical reference tools, *see* Joseph D. Allison, *Bible Study Resource Guide* (Nashville: Thomas Nelson, 1982).

4. "How Knowing Greek Led Me to Know God," as told by Nicholas Kip, *Awake!* (March 22, 1987), 10–14.

## Chapter 1  The Eternal Person of the Word

1. *See* Jerald and Sandra Tanner, *The Changing World of Mormonism* (Chicago: Moody Press, 1980), 383–395, for a discussion of the *Inspired Version* and its rendering of John 1:1.

2. Victor Paul Wierwille, *Jesus Christ Is Not God* (New Knoxville, OH: American Christian Press, 1971), 85. For an evangelical critical analysis, *see* Robert Sumner, *Jesus Christ IS God!* (Murfreesboro, TN: Biblical Evangelism Press, 1985).

3. For a brief overview and critique of Armstrong's theology, *see* this author's review article, *"Mystery of the Ages:* A Summary Critique," *Christian Research Journal* 9, 3 (Winter 1987). For a thorough refutation of the doctrine that men can become "God" or "gods," *see* this author's "Ye Are Gods? Orthodox and Heretical Views on the Deification of Man," in the same issue of the *CRJ* (formerly known as *Forward;* available from Christian Research Institute, P.O. Box 500, San Juan Capistrano, CA 92693).

4. Mary Baker Eddy, *Miscellaneous Writings 1883–1896* (Boston: Trustees under the Will of Mary Baker G. Eddy, 1896), 29.

5. Mary Baker Eddy, *The First Church of Christ Scientist and Miscellany* (Boston: Trustees under the Will of Mary Baker G. Eddy, 1913), 117.

6. For a general refutation of Oneness Pentecostal teaching, *see* this author's "Oneness Pentecostalism and the Trinity: A Biblical Critique," *Forward* 8, 3 (Fall 1985):22–27.

7. In 1962 the Watchtower published a booklet which mentioned in passing that a 1904 book called *The Patristic Gospels: An English Version of the Holy Gospels as they existed in the Second Century,* by Roslyn D'Onston, claimed in a note that the true reading of John 1:1 "probably" should be "of God" *(theou)* instead of "God" *(theos),* so that John 1:1c would have read, "and the Word was of God" *("The Word"—Who Was He? According to John* [Watchtower Bible and Tract Society (hereafter WTBTS), 1962], 53–54). Yet the booklet goes on to ignore that claim and discusses John 1:1 on the assumption that the text did originally read *kai theos ēn ho logos,* and subsequent discussions of John 1:1 in Watchtower publications have invariably assumed the accuracy of the Greek text. Since D'Onston's arguments were based on speculation and not hard evidence, and since even the JWs evidently recognize that the text as we have it is genuine, we are safe in ignoring the proposed textual emendation.

8. The Septuagint was a translation of the Hebrew-Aramaic Old Testament into Greek produced by Greek-speaking Jews in the third century B.C. It was used a great deal by the writers of the New Testament. It was called the "Septuagint" because it was supposedly translated by seventy men (thus the abbreviation LXX).

9. *New World Translation of the Holy Scriptures: With References* [hereafter NWT (1984)] (WTBTS, 1984), 1281. The cross-reference to "beginning" in Genesis 1:1 lists only one text, Hebrews 1:10 (NWT [1984], 15). Ironically, Hebrews 1:10 is speaking of the eternality of Christ!

10. The parallel was not always noticeable in the NWT; in the first edition of the New Testament portion of the NWT, *en archē* in John 1:1 was

translated "Originally." Some JWs even used to argue from this rendering that the Word had an "origin"; and today some JWs argue that the mere presence of the word *beginning* in John 1:1 proves that the Word had a beginning (whereas, as we are seeking to demonstrate, John's point is the exact opposite).

11. Herle, *The Trinity Doctrine,* 36.

12. On this subject *see* Hugh Ross, "Cosmology Confronts Christ, the Creator" (Reasons to Believe, 1987 rev. ed.; available from P.O. Box 5978, Pasadena, CA 91107).

13. A. T. Robertson, *A Grammar of the Greek New Testament in the Light of Historical Research* (Nashville: Broadman Press, 1934), 883; cited in Herle, 37.

14. *The Watchtower* (May 15, 1977), 319.

15. *Reasoning from the Scriptures* (WTBTS, 1985), 416.

16. *"The Word"—Who Is He? According to John* (WTBTS, 1962), 6.

# Chapter 2 The Case of the Missing Article

1. *Aid to Bible Understanding* (WTBTS, 1971), 1207.

2. Ed. L. Miller, "'The *Logos* was God,'" *Evangelical Quarterly* 53, 2 (1981):68.

3. Bruce Vawter, "The Gospel According to John," *Jerome Biblical Commentary,* ed. Raymond E. Brown, et. al. (Englewood Cliffs, NJ: Prentice-Hall, 1969), 422.

4. Bruce Vawter, *The Four Gospels: An Introduction* (Garden City, NY: Doubleday & Co., 1967), 39.

5. Harner, "Qualitative Anarthrous Predicate Nouns," 86–87.

6. A. T. Robertson, *Word Pictures in the New Testament* (Nashville: Broadman Press, 1932), 4–5.

7. That is, against the view that John 1:1 reflects the first-century Hellenistic Jewish philosopher Philo's distinction between *theos* and *ho theos,* a view which Dodd concludes does not fit the evidence of the Gospel of John. This is because, as Dodd points out, the anarthrous *theos* is frequently used in John with no detectable variation of meaning from *ho theos.*

8. C. H. Dodd, "New Testament Translation Problems II," *The Bible Translator* 28, 1 (Jan. 1977):103.

9. *See,* for example, Ernest de Witt Burton, *Syntax of the Moods and Tenses in New Testament Greek,* 3rd ed. (Edinburgh: T. & T. Clark, 1898); K. J. Dover, *Greek Word Order* (Cambridge, Eng.: Cambridge University Press, 1960); William Watson Goodwin, *Syntax of the Moods and Tenses of the Greek Verb* (New York: St. Martin's Press, 1965); R. W. Moore, *Comparative Greek and Latin Syntax* (London: G. Bell and Sons, 1934); and James Hope

Moulton, *A Grammar of New Testament Greek*, Vol. 3, *Syntax*, by Nigel
Turner (Edinburgh: T. & T. Clark, 1963).

## Chapter 3  Definite or Indefinite?

1. Maximilian Zerwick, *Biblical Greek: Illustrated by Examples*, Eng. ed.
adapted from the 4th Latin ed. by Joseph Smith, S.J. (Rome: Scripta Pon-
tificii Instituti Biblici, 1963), 53.
2. For documentation of this frequent error in JW literature, *see* especially Duane Magnani, *The Watchtower Files* (Minneapolis: Bethany
House Publishers, 1985), 133–139.
3. On John 20:28, *see* Appendix A of this book. On Titus 2:13, 2 Peter
1:1, and 1 John 5:20, see this author's "Sharp's Rule and the Deity of
Christ" (unpublished manuscript, available from Christian Research Institute). It is also possible that in Acts 20:28 and Romans 9:5 Christ is called
*ho theos*, but the former is strongly disputed as to the translation, while the
latter, though almost certainly calling Jesus *theos*, has the definite article
more clearly attached to *ōn epi pantōn* ("being over all") that to *theos*. On
Romans 9:5, see especially Bruce M. Metzger, "The Punctuation of Rom.
9:5," in *Christ and Spirit in the New Testament: In Honour of Charles Francis
Digby Moule*, edited by Barnabas Lindars and Stephen S. Smalley
(Cambridge, Eng.: Cambridge University Press, 1973), 95–112.
4. A good example is Leonard Hillstrom's statement, "Nothing is indefinite about the predicate nominative *theos*" in John 1:1. Leonard H.
Hillstrom, "A Selective Study of the Greek Article in the New Testament,"
Th.M. thesis (Western Conservative Baptist Seminary, 1967), 66.
5. Harner, "Qualitative Anathrous Predicate Nouns," 75.
6. NWT (1984), 1579, compare with Herle (1983 ed.), 35.
7. Ibid., 36.
8. Ibid., 34.
9. The lists in this chapter, taken together, are almost identical to the
list given by Daniel B. Wallace, "The Semantics and Exegetical Significance of the Object-Complement Construction in the New Testament,"
*Grace Theological Journal* 6, 1 (1985), 107 n. 71. There are, however, some
differences. A complete list should be available soon from D. A. Carson of
Trinity Evangelical Divinity School in his forthcoming grammatical concordance to the New Testament that will utilize a computer program
called GRAMCORD.
10. The meaning of the words *Son of Man* in the sayings of Jesus is
widely debated among scholars, and there does not seem to be any end in
sight to the debate. Recently the debate has focused on the significance, if
any, of the use of the definite articles (since usually the expression reads in
Greek, "the Son of the Man"). For those wishing to see what this debate is

all about, *see* the following article (which this writer does not endorse) and the sources cited in its notes: P. Maurice Casey, "General, Generic and Indefinite: The Use of the Term 'Son of Man' in Aramaic Sources and in the Teaching of Jesus," *Journal for the Study of the New Testament* 29 (1987):21–56.

## Chapter 4   The Word: "God" or "a God"?

1. For an example of this argument in Watchtower literature, see *The Watchtower* 104, 23 (Dec. 1, 1983), 14.

2. Michael Van Buskirk, *The Scholastic Dishonesty of the Watchtower* (Santa Ana, CA: CARIS, 1976), 17, 18. This booklet is out of print.

3. Compare Daniel B. Wallace, "The Semantics and Exegetical Significance of the Object-Complement Construction in the New Testament," *Grace Theological Journal* 6, 1 (1985):91–112.

4. *The Watchtower* (Dec. 1, 1983), 14.

5. *See* n. 3.

## Chapter 5   Scholars' Words about the Word in John 1:1

1. E. C. Colwell, "A Definite Rule for the Use of the Article in the Greek New Testament," *Journal of Biblical Literature* 52 (1933):12–21.

2. For a sympathetic overview of Colwell's article (which does not fully recognize its limitations as relating to John 1:1), *see* Robert H. Countess, *The Jehovah's Witnesses' New Testament: A Critical Analysis of the New World Translation of the Christian Greek Scriptures* (Phillipsburg, NJ: Presbyterian & Reformed, 1982), 48–54. Even Countess notes that "an anarthrous predicate noun is indefinite in this position only if demanded by the context" (53)—which shows that such nouns can be indefinite. Countess's book is actually a reprint of his 1966 dissertation. For a more recent and more critical (though brief) discussion see D. A. Carson, *Exegetical Fallacies* (Grand Rapids: Baker Book House, 1984), 86–88.

3. Colwell, 13.

4. Ibid., 18–19.

5. Ibid., 20.

6. Robert W. Funk, "The Syntax of the Greek Article: Its Importance for Critical Pauline Problems," Ph.D. diss. (Nashville: Vanderbilt University Divinity School, 1953).

7. Lane C. McGaughy, *Toward a Descriptive Analysis of 'EINAI as a Linking Verb in New Testament Greek*, Ph.D. diss., Vanderbilt University, SBL Dissertation Series, No. 6 (Missoula, MT: Society of Biblical Literature, 1972).

8. Ibid., 74–75.

9. For example, Carson, 87; P. S. Dixon, "The Significance of the Anarthrous Predicate Nominative in John," Th.M. thesis (Dallas: Dallas Theological Seminary, 1975); Daniel B. Wallace, "The Semantics and Exegetical Significance of the Object-Complement Construction in the New Testament," *Grace Theological Journal* 6, 1 (1985):106–107.

10. Colwell, 20–21.

11. Ibid., 21.

12. Ibid.

13. Recently, this JW sent me a letter requesting that I not mention his name in any of my writings, for unstated "personal" reasons.

14. Philip B. Harner, "Qualitative Anarthrous Predicate Nouns: Mark 15:39 and John 1:1," *Journal of Biblical Literature* 92, 1 (March 1973):75–87.

15. Ibid., 87.

16. *See especially* NWT (1984), 1579; also Herle, 29, 33.

17. *Reasoning from the Scriptures,* 212.

18. Harner, 87.

19. Ibid., 86–87.

20. Ibid., 84.

21. Ibid., 85. (The next several quotations from Harner's article are also from this page.)

22. Ibid., 86; *see* above, p. 35 and n. 5.

23. Ibid., 87.

24. Ernst Haenchen, *John 1: A Commentary on the Gospel of John, Chapters 1–6,* trans. by Robert W. Funk, ed. by Robert W. Funk with Ulrich Busse (Philadelphia: Fortress Press, 1984), hereafter "Funk (1984)."

25. Haenchen, *Das Johannesevangelium. Ein Kommentar,* aus den nachgelassenen Manuskripten, herausgegeben von Ulrich Busse, mit einem Vorwort von James M. Robinson (Tubingen: J.C.B. Mohr [Paul Siebeck], 1980), hereafter "Haenchen."

26. Funk (1984), 108.

27. Haenchen, 112.

28. As Funk himself translates it elsewhere (Funk [1984], 110).

29. Funk (1984), 109.

30. Haenchen, 116.

31. Funk (1984), 109.

32. Ibid.

33. Ibid.

34. Funk (1984), 110. "Patripassianism" refers to the heresy that the person who died on the cross was the Father—that is, a form of modalism.

35. Ibid.

36. Ibid.

37. Harner (see n. 14).

38. Haenchen, 112–115.

39. *The Watchtower* (May 15, 1977):320.

40. William Barclay, *Many Witnesses, One Lord* (Grand Rapids: Baker Book House, 1973), 23, 24.

41. Ibid., 23.

42. Letter from Barclay to Donald P. Shoemaker, August 26, 1977. Photocopies of the *Watchtower* article, the passage in Barclay's book, and Barclay's letter, can all be found in Randall Watters, *Thus Saith . . . the Governing Body of Jehovah's Witnesses* (Manhattan Beach, CA: Bethel Ministries, 1984), 72–74.

43. *Reasoning from the Scriptures*, 416–17.

44. Herle, *Trinity Doctrine*, 30.

45. *Reasoning from the Scriptures*, 417. The book notes that McKenzie's work was published "with nihil obstat and imprimatur," official guarantees that the work conforms to Roman Catholic doctrine. This should have suggested to the Society that this sentence must be out of context, since the Catholic church is staunchly trinitarian and would never give its imprimatur to a book that denied Christ's deity.

46. John L. McKenzie, *Dictionary of the Bible* (New York: Macmillan, 1965), 317.

47. Ibid.

48. Henry Alford, *Alford's Greek Testament: An Exegetical and Critical Commentary,* Vol. I, Part II: *Luke-John* (Grand Rapids: Guardian Press, 1976 reprint of 1854 ed.), 681.

49. C. K. Barrett, *The Gospel According to St. John* (London: SPCK, 1955), 76.

50. Dodd, "New Testament Translation Problems II," 104.

51. Bruce M. Metzger, "The Jehovah's Witnesses and Jesus Christ," *Theology Today* (April 1953):75.

52. James Moffatt, *Jesus Christ the Same* (Nashville: Abingdon-Cokesbury, 1945), 61.

53. A. T. Robertson, *A Grammar of the Greek New Testament in the Light of Historical Research* (Nashville: Broadman Press, 1932), 767. Notice that Robertson states forthrightly that *theos* in John 1:1 is indefinite, yet also affirms that the Word is called "God" (see n. 54). On "distributed" and "undistributed," *see* chapter 2.

54. A. T. Robertson and W. Hersey Davis, *A New Short Grammar of the Greek Testament,* 10th ed. (Grand Rapids: Baker Book House, 1977), 279.

55. B. F. Westcott, *The Gospel According to St. John* (Grand Rapids: William B. Eerdmans, 1958 reprint), 3.

## Chapter 6     Past, Present, and Perfect

1. St. Athanasius, "Four Discourses Against the Arians" (I.iv.13), in *A Select Library of Nicene and Post-Nicene Fathers of the Christian Church*, Second Series, edited by Philip Schaff and Henry Wace, Vol. IV (Grand Rapids: William B. Eerdmans Publishing Co., 1953), 314.

2. John Calvin, *Calvin: Institutes of the Christian Religion*, ed. John T. McNeill, tr. and indexed by Ford Lewis Battles; Library of Christian Classics Vols. XX and XXI (Philadelphia: Westminster Press, 1960), Vol. 1, 483 (*Institutes* II.xiv.2). Battles notes that Calvin was thinking especially of Michael Servetus (483, n. 5).

3. For discussions of Grotius's and Socinus's interpretations, see Hermann Olshausen, *Biblical Commentary on the New Testament*, trans. from the German, Vol. II (New York: Sheldon & Co., 1860), 465; and Heinrich August Wilhelm Meyer, *Critical and Exegetical Hand-book to the Gospel of John*, trans. from the German (New York: Funk & Wagnalls, 1884), 293. This sort of interpretation of John 8:58 has been revived in an altered form among the "Jesus Only" Oneness Pentecostals, some of whom argue that Jesus meant that God planned from eternity to become man, not that he preexisted Abraham as a second person alongside the Father. For a biblical refutation of this teaching, see this author's "Oneness Pentecostalism and the Trinity: A Biblical Critique," *Forward* (Fall 1985):22–27.

4. J. Ernest Davey, *The Jesus of St. John: Historical and Christological Studies in the Fourth Gospel* (London: Lutterworth Press, 1958), 136.

5. Any of the better recent commentaries on John discusses these points in detail; see also the chapter on John in Donald Guthrie, *New Testament Introduction* (Downers Grove, IL: InterVarsity Press, 1970).

6. *Kingdom Interlinear Translation of the Greek Scriptures* (WTBTS, 1985 rev. ed.; hereafter cited as KIT), 451, left column.

7. "Questions from Readers," *The Watchtower* (Feb. 15, 1957):126–127 (hereafter cited as "Questions").

8. NWT (1950), at John 8:58.

9. Walter Martin, *The Kingdom of the Cults* (Minneapolis: Bethany House, 1977), 77–78. In the 1985 revised edition, the last sentence quoted was changed slightly to read, "The term 'perfect indefinite' is not a standard grammatical term, and its use here has been invented by the authors of the note, so it is impossible to know what is meant" (88, rev. ed.). This wording reflects the fact that in the late 1970s Nelson Herle brought to Martin's attention two English grammars that did in fact contain the term *perfect indefinite*, although not with the same meaning as the JWs attach to it (on this point, see further in this chapter).

10. "Questions," 126.

11. NWT (1963 large print ed.), at John 8:58.

12. KIT (1985 rev. ed.), at John 8:58.

13. KIT (1969 ed.), at John 8:58.

14. Herle, 43–44, 48–49.

15. This erroneous teaching is based on a misunderstanding of Proverbs 4:18, "But the path of the righteous ones is like the bright light that is getting lighter and lighter until the day is firmly established" (NWT). The point of the passage is that their conduct becomes more and more conformed to God's will, not that truth is revealed progressively—and certainly not that what was once taught as fact can be contradicted or laid aside by "new light." Even Charles Taze Russell, founder of the Jehovah's Witnesses, admitted as much (*Zion's Watch Tower* [Feb. 1881], 188). The Society's attempt to evade this problem by speaking of "tacking into the wind" does not solve the problem (*The Watchtower* [Dec. 1, 1981], 27), as that particular maneuver never involves going *backward*.

16. Letter from the Watchtower Bible and Tract Society to Firpo W. Carr, February 7, 1978.

17. Martin (1977 ed.), 77–78; Michael Van Buskirk, *The Scholastic Dishonesty of the Watchtower* (Costa Mesa, CA: CARIS, 1976), 17, 20.

18. Letter of Nelson A. Herle, Jr., to Dr. Walter R. Martin, March 8, 1982. In a letter to Herle dated July 8, 1981, Martin had made the statement, "In the 1950 edition of the *New World Translation* and the footnote of John 8:58, it was clearly stated that the perfect indefinite tense was in the Greek language." It must be said that the footnote was not explicit on this point, and could most easily be interpreted as Herle has argued. On the other hand, when the NWT was first published, many Jehovah's Witnesses, including members of the staff at the Jehovah's Witnesses' headquarters in Brooklyn, New York ("Bethel"), considered the term *perfect indefinite tense* to refer to a Greek tense. (One such Witness, who has now become a Christian, was Bill Cetnar, who worked at Bethel in the early 1950s.) It has only been since 1977, when Nelson Herle began publicizing his find that two old English grammars used the term, that the Witnesses have argued that it referred to an English tense. Nevertheless, it may be granted that the author of the footnote *may* have had an English tense in mind, though the Watchtower Society never bothered to say so and document its existence for almost thirty years after Walter Martin first accused them of making the term up. In any case, Nelson Herle is in error in claiming that the Society used the term as it was found in English grammars (see further below).

19. Herle, *Trinity*, 50.

20. See n. 16.

21. Maurice H. Weseen, *Crowell's Dictionary of English Grammar and Handbook of American Usage* (New York: Thomas Y. Crowell, 1928); Henry

Sweet, *A New English Grammar Logical and Historical* (Oxford: Clarendon Press, 1900); hereafter cited as Weseen and as Sweet.

22. Weseen, 177.

23. See n. 19.

24. Sweet, 105; Weseen, 178.

25. Letter from Herle to Walter Martin, March 7, 1979, 2.

26. Quite recently the Society has apparently begun making use of Herle's find. In a letter from the Watchtower Bible and Tract Society of Canada, dated December 26, 1985, to a Mr. Jack Tolland, Sweet and Weseen are both cited as indicating "that there is a perfect definite tense and a perfect indefinite tense." The fact that these are the same two grammars used by Herle makes it fairly certain that this information was borrowed by the Society from Herle.

## Chapter 7   Jesus Christ: Eternal, or Just Very Old?

1. "Questions," 126.

2. For example, at a meeting on June 29, 1984, Nelson Herle admitted in passing that John 8:58 was not an historical present. At another meeting, on January 15, 1987, Herle and several other JWs were challenged to admit openly that John 8:58 was not an historical present. One JW, who was a graduate student in Greek, responded, "I wouldn't put it that way," a cautious response indeed. Herle, however, quietly stated, "It's not an historical present." It is interesting to note that the JWs refused in advance to allow the meeting to be tape recorded, probably for the very reason that they did not wish such admissions to be recorded.

3. *Reasoning from the Scriptures* (WTBTS, 1985), 136–137. For additional evidence that they do *not* freely admit error, see this author's article, "The Whitewashing of the Watchtower," *Forward* 9 (Summer 1986):9–14, published by Christian Research Institute.

4. Letter from the Watchtower Bible and Tract Society to Firpo W. Carr, February 7, 1978. Moreover, one JW published an article in 1971 in which he repeated more or less verbatim the argument of the 1957 *Watchtower* concerning the historical present; *see* Dennis W. Light, "Some Observations on the New World Translation," *The Bible Collector* 7, 27–28 (July-Dec. 1971):8–9.

5. *See* "Questions," 127.

6. A. T. Robertson, *A Grammar of the Greek New Testament in the Light of Historical Research* (Nashville, TN: Broadman Press, 1934), 866–68.

7. Ibid.; Nigel Turner, *Syntax*, Vol. III of *A Grammar of New Testament Greek*, ed. James Hope Moulton (Edinburgh: T. & T. Clark, 1963), 62.

8. See n. 6.

9. *Funk and Wagnalls Standard Desk Dictionary*, Vol. 1 (n.p.: Funk and Wagnalls, 1983), 305.

10. Robert W. Funk, *A Beginning-Intermediate Grammar of Hellenistic Greek,* Vol. II: *Syntax;* 2nd. ed. (Missoula, MT: Society of Biblical Literature, 1973), 614.

11. "Questions," 126–127.

12. Ibid.

13. Charles Fox Burney, *The Aramaic Origin of the Fourth Gospel* (Oxford: Clarendon Press, 1922), 87.

14. Harry Sturz, "Observations on the New World Translation," *The Bible Collector* 7, 27–28 (July-Dec. 1971):13. More recently, Daniel B. Wallace has argued that historical presents occur only with third person verbs (which would eliminate *eimi,* since it is in the first person, that is, "I" instead of "he"), and never with a linking verb: Daniel B. Wallace, *Selected Notes on the Syntax of New Testament Greek,* 4th ed. (Winona Lake, IN: Grace Theological Seminary, 1981), 182–87.

15. Turner, 60; *see also* Friedrich Wilhelm Blass and Albert Debrunner, *A Greek Grammar of the New Testament and Other Early Christian Literature,* tr. and rev. by Robert W. Funk (Chicago: University of Chicago Press, 1961), 167.

16. Robertson, *A Grammar,* 866–68.

17. Letter from Herle to Walter R. Martin, April 2, 1978, 2.

18. Herle, *Trinity,* 44.

19. NWT (1984), 1582–83.

20. KIT (1985), 1145.

21. Winer and Turner appear to be the only Greek grammarians who identify it as such. The only twentieth-century commentary that identifies John 8:58 as a PPA appears to be Sanders and Mastin (see n. 41 below).

22. Georg Benedict Winer, *A Grammar of the Idiom of the New Testament,* 7th ed., enlarged and improved by Gottlieb Lunemann (Andover, MA: Warren F. Draper, 1897), 267.

23. Turner, 62.

24. This cautious form of the argument, which does not claim that the orthodox interpretation is ruled out by the use of the PPA, was used in letters to this writer from Hal Flemings, a JW living in southern California.

25. Herle, 50.

26. Ernest De Witt Burton, *Syntax of the Moods and Tenses of New Testament Greek,* 2nd ed. (Chicago: University of Chicago Press, 1900), 10 (sect. 17).

27. Ibid.

28. William Waston Goodwin, *Greek Grammar,* revised by Charles Burton Gulick (Waltham, MA: Blaisdell Publishing Co., 1958), 268 (sect. 1258a).

29. Harvey Eugene Dana and Julius R. Mantey, *A Manual Grammar of the Greek New Testament* (Toronto: Macmillan, 1957), 183.

30. Robertson, *A Grammar,* 879.

31. NWT (1984), 1579.

32. Letter of Nelson A. Herle, Jr., to Walter R. Martin, April 2, 1978, p. 2.

33. Unfortunately, there is a minor textual question here. The KIT Greek text has the present tense *zētoumen*, while the United Bible Societies' *Greek New Testament* has the imperfect *ezētoumen* (and does not even list *zētoumen* as a textual variant). However, even the present tense *zētoumen* would here not be a PPA, because there is no adverbial clause expressing duration.

34. Robertson, 880.

35. The term *predicate absolute* is a formal expression used for this grammatical phenomenon, which occurs so rarely that there is no separate discussion of it in the major New Testament Greek grammars; exegetes frequently refer to it more simply as an "absolute use" of the verb. Its significance has been discussed, for example, by Mark L. Appold, *The Oneness Motif in the Fourth Gospel: Motif Analysis and Exegetical Probe into the Theology of John* (Tubingen: J. C. B. Mohr, 1976), 81–82; William Barclay, *Introduction to John and the Acts of the Apostles* (Philadelphia: Westminster Press, 1976), 117–18; Raymond E. Brown, "The *Egō Eimi* ('I Am') Passages in the Fourth Gospel," in *A Companion to John: Readings in Johannine Theology,* ed. by Michael J. Taylor (Staten Island, NY: Alba House, 1977), 117; et. al.

36. Martin, 1977 ed., 78 (1985 ed., 88).

37. See n. 32.

38. Herle, *Trinity,* 45.

39. Burton, 10 (sect. 17).

40. Herle, 50.

41. J. N. Sanders, *A Commentary on the Gospel According to St. John,* ed. and completed by B. A. Mastin, Harper's New Testament Commentaries (New York: Harper & Row, 1968), 236.

42. Sanders, 148.

43. Augustine of Hippo, "Homilies on the Gospel of John," tr. John Gibb, *A Select Library of the Nicene and Post-Nicene Fathers of the Christian Church,* ed. Philip Schaff, Vol. VII (Grand Rapids: William B. Eerdmans Publishing Co., 1978; orig. pub. 1888), 244 (XLIII.17).

44. Henry Alford, *Alford's Greek Testament: An Exegetical and Critical Commentary,* Vol. I, Part II: Luke-John (Grand Rapids: Guardian Press, 1976 reprint of 1854 ed.), 802; William Barclay, *The Gospel of John,* Vol. 2; Daily Study Bible; rev. ed. (Philadelphia: Westminster Press, 1975), 36; Charles Kingsley Barrett, *The Gospel According to St. John,* 2nd ed. (Philadelphia: Westminster Press, 1978), 352; Friedrich Buchsel, *"eimi, ho ōn,"* *Theological Dictionary of the New Testament,* Vol. II, ed. Gerhard Kittel, tr. Geoffrey W. Bromiley (Grand Rapids: William B. Eerdmans Publishing

Co., 1964), 399; Rudolf Bultmann, *The Gospel of John: A Commentary,* tr. by G. R. Beasley-Murray, genl. ed., and by R. W. N. Hoare and J. K. Riches (Philadelphia: Westminster Press, 1971), 327 n. 4; Charles Harold Dodd, *The Interpretation of the Fourth Gospel* (Cambridge, Eng.: Cambridge University Press, 1953), 261; R. C. H. Lenski, *The Interpretation of St. John's Gospel* (Columbus, OH: The Wartburg Press, 1942), 670; Barnabas Lindars, *The Gospel of John,* New Century Bible (London: Oliphants, 1972), 336; A. T. Robertson, *Word Pictures in the New Testament,* Vol. V (New York: Harper & Brothers, 1932), 158–59; Rudolf Schnackenburg, *The Gospel According to St. John,* 3 Vols. (New York: Seabury Press—Crossroad Books, 1980), Vol. 2, 80, 223; Marvin R. Vincent, *Word Studies in the New Testament* (New York: Charles Scribner's Sons, 1914), 181; Brooke Foss Westcott, *The Gospel According to St. John* (Grand Rapids: William B. Eerdmans Publishing Co., 1954 reprint of 1908 ed.), 28.

45. "The *egō* which Jesus speaks as the Revealer is the 'I' of the eternal Logos, which was in the beginning, the 'I' of the eternal God himself." Bultmann, 327.

46. Davey, 136 (see above, pp. 88–89).

47. Schnackenburg, 224.

48. Frederick Louis Godet, *Commentary on the Gospel of John,* Classic Commentary Library (Grand Rapids: Zondervan Publishing Co., reprint of 1893 ed.), trans. from the 3rd French ed. by Timothy Dwight, pp. 357–58, and citing Christoph Ernst Luthardt, *St. John's Gospel: Described and Explained According to Its Peculiar Character,* tr. Caspar Rene Gregory (Edinburgh: T. & T. Clark, 1877).

## Chapter 8   "I Am" as the Words of Jehovah

1. Edwin Hatch and Henry A. Redpath, *A Concordance to the Septuagint and the Other Greek Versions of the Old Testament (including the Apocryphal Books),* Vol. II (Graz, Austria: Akademische Druck—U. Verlagsanstalt, 1954), 1203.

2. For example, *Aid to Bible Understanding,* 665; *You Can Live Forever in Paradise on Earth* (WTBTS, 1982), 44.

3. Albert Barnes, *Notes on the New Testament Explanatory and Practical: Luke and John* (Grand Rapids: Baker Book House, 1977 reprint), 276; Barrett, 352; Raymond E. Brown, *The Gospel According to John (i-xii),* Anchor Bible (Garden City, NY: Doubleday & Co., 1966), 360; Bultmann, 327 n. 4; Godet, 356; Ernst Wilhelm Hengstenberg, *Commentary on the Gospel of St. John* (Edinburgh: T. & T. Clark, 1865), Vol. I, 474; Edwyn Clement Hoskyns, *The Fourth Gospel,* ed. Francis Noel Davey (London: Faber and Faber, 1947), 349; Lindars, 336; William Milligan and William F. Moulton, *Commentary on the Gospel of St. John* (Edinburgh: T. & T. Clark, 1898), 111;

Alfred Plummer, *The Gospel According to S. John*, Cambridge Greek Testament for Schools (Cambridge, England: Cambridge University Press, 1900), 202; Robertson, *Word Pictures*, 159; Schnackenburg, 223; Winer, 267.

4. Letters from Firpo Carr and Nelson Herle to this author.

5. Daniel P. Fuller, *Hermeneutics* (Pasadena: Fuller Theological Seminary, 1978), ch. IX, 14–16.

6. William David Davies, *The Gospel and the Land: Early Christianity and Jewish Territorial Doctrine* (Berkeley: University of California Press, 1974), 290–296; Ethelbert Stauffer, *Jesus and His Story*, trans. by Richard and Clara Winston (New York: Alfred A. Knopf, 1960), 174–195; and especially Philip B. Harner, *The "I Am" of the Fourth Gospel: A Study in Johannine Usage and Thought* (Philadelphia: Fortress Press, 1970).

7. NWT (1984), 1583.

8. Joseph Crehan, *The Theology of St. John* (London: Darton, Longman and Todd, 1960), 93.

9. In this author's correspondence with Nelson Herle, Firpo Carr, and others, this was practically the only issue with respect to John 8:58 that they would discuss, other than that text's relationship to Psalm 90:2. Neither Herle nor Carr even attempted to disprove the force of eternality in *eimi* in John 8:58. This is probably because it is easier to dispute a connection between two separate texts than to dispute a grammatically sound interpretation of one of those texts.

10. Herle, *Trinity Doctrine*, 42.

11. Olshausen, *Biblical Commentary*, 464–465.

12. *Reasoning from the Scriptures*, 418.

13. Barrett, 352 (see also 342–51).

14. Herle, 42.

15. *See*, for example, Merrill C. Tenney, "The Gospel of John," *The Expositor's Bible Commentary*, ed. Frank E. Gaebelein, Vol. 9 (Grand Rapids: Zondervan, 1981), 99.

16. NWT (1950), 312 fn. c; NWT (1984), 186.

17. NWT (1984), 86, 1583.

18. Charles R. Gianotti, "The Meaning of the Divine Name YHWH," *Bibliotheca Sacra* (Jan.-March 1985):38–51.

19. See n. 9.

20. D. A. Carson, *Exegetical Fallacies* (Grand Rapids: Baker Book House, 1984), 44–45; Moises Silva, *Biblical Words and Their Meaning: An Introduction to Lexical Semantics* (Grand Rapids: Zondervan Publishing Co., 1983), 18–34.

21. Walther Zimmerli, *Old Testament Theology in Outline* (Atlanta: John Knox Press, 1978), 20, 21.

22. Gianotti, 41.

23. Ibid., 38–39.

24. *See especially* Robert Countess, *The Jehovah's Witnesses' New Testament* (Phillipsburg, NJ: Presbyterian & Reformed, 1982), and Doug Mason,

*JEHOVAH in the Jehovah's Witnesses' New World Translation* (Doug Mason, 1987; available from Bethel Ministries, CP-258, Manhattan Beach, CA).

25. See n. 10.

26. Davey, 94; Leon Morris, *The Gospel According to John*, New International Commentary on the New Testament (Grand Rapids: William B. Eerdmans Publishing Co., 1971), 473; Alan Richardson, *The Gospel According to Saint John*, Torch Bible Commentaries (London: SCM Press, 1959), 118; Sanders, 236 n. 2; Schnackenburg, 84, 224; Robert Harvey Strachan, *The Fourth Gospel: Its Significance and Environment*, 3rd rev. ed. (London: SCM Press, 1941), 19–21; R. V. G. Tasker, *The Gospel According to St. John*, Tyndale New Testament Commentaries (Grand Rapids: William B. Eerdmans Publishing Co., 1960), 122.

27. Barrett, 352.

28. Bultmann, 327 n. 5 (continued to 328).

29. Lindars, 336.

30. Bultmann, 327 n. 5 (found on 328).

31. William Temple, *Readings in St. John's Gospel*, First and Second Series (London: Macmillan & Co., 1945), 149–150.

32. Letter of a JW who wishes to remain anonymous, to this author, dated January 25, 1985.


## Appendix A    John 20:28

1. C. F. D. Moule, *An Idiom Book of New Testament Greek* (Cambridge, Eng.: Cambridge University Press, 1953), 116.

2. *Aid to Bible Understanding* (WTBTS, 1971), 885.


## Appendix B    How Scholars Have Translated John 1:1

1. JW citations of these translations can be found in Herle, *The Trinity Doctrine*, 32; NWT (1984), 1579; *Reasoning from the Scriptures*, 212, 417; "The Word"—*Who Is He? According to John*, 4–5, 56; KIT (1985), 1139.

2. Cited in Herle, 32.

3. For complete documentation on the JWs' use of Johannes Greber, contact Duane Magnani, Witness, Inc., P.O. Box 597, Clayton, CA 94517.


## Appendix C    How Scholars Have Translated John 8:58

1. Herle, *The Trinity Doctrine*, 48–49.

# Select Bibliography

Bowman, Robert M., Jr. "The Whitewashing of the Watchtower," *Forward* 9, 1 (Summer 1986):9–14.

Brown, Raymond E. *The Gospel According to John (i-xii)*, Anchor Bible (Garden City, NY: Doubleday & Co., 1966).

Buchsel, Friedrich. *"eimi, ho ōn,"* *Theological Dictionary of the New Testament*, Vol. II, ed. Gerhard Kittel, tr. Geoffrey W. Bromiley (Grand Rapids: William B. Eerdmans Publishing Co., 1964), 398–400.

Carson, D. A. *Exegetical Fallacies* (Grand Rapids: Baker Book House, 1984).

Colwell, E. C. "A Definite Rule for the Use of the Article in the Greek New Testament," *Journal of Biblical Literature* 52 (1933):12–21.

Countess, Robert H. *The Jehovah's Witnesses' New Testament: A Critical Analysis of the New World Translation of the Christian Greek Scriptures* (Phillipsburg, NJ: Presbyterian & Reformed, 1982).

Dodd, Charles Harold. "New Testament Translation Problems II," *The Bible Translator* 28, 1 (Jan. 1977):101–16.

Harner, Philip B. *The "I Am" of the Fourth Gospel: A Study in Johannine Usage and Thought* (Philadelphia: Fortress Press, 1970).

———. "Qualitative Anarthrous Predicate Nouns: Mark 15:39 and John 1:1," *Journal of Biblical Literature* 92, 1 (March 1973):75–87.

Herle, Nelson A., Jr. *The Trinity Doctrine Examined in the Light of History and the Bible*, unpub. manuscript (1983; rev. ed. 1987). [JW]

Kip, Nicholas. "How Knowing Greek Led Me to Know God," *Awake!* (March 22, 1987), 10–14. [JW]

Lenski, R. C. H. *The Interpretation of St. John's Gospel* (Columbus, OH: The Wartburg Press, 1942; orig. 1931).

Magnani, Duane. *The Watchtower Files* (Minneapolis: Bethany House Publishers, 1985).

Martin, Walter R. *The Kingdom of the Cults*, 5th ed. (Minneapolis: Bethany House Publishers, 1985).

McGaughy, Lane C. *Toward a Descriptive Analysis of 'EINAI as a Linking Verb in New Testament Greek*, Ph.D. diss., Vanderbilt University; SBL Dissertation Series, No. 6 (Missoula, MT: Society of Biblical Literature, 1972).

Miller, Ed. L. "The *Logos* Was God," *Evangelical Quarterly* 53, 2 (1981):65–77.

Morris, Leon. *The Gospel According to John*, New International Commentary on the New Testament (Grand Rapids: William B. Eerdmans Publishing Co., 1971).

Sire, James. *Scripture Twisting* (Downers Grove, IL: InterVarsity Press, 1980).

Stauffer, Ethelbert. *Jesus and His Story*, tr. Richard and Clara Winston (New York: Alfred A. Knopf, 1960), 174–195.

Wallace, Daniel B. "The Semantics and Exegetical Significance of the Object-Complement Construction in the New Testament," *Grace Theological Journal* 6, 1 (1985):91–112.

Watchtower Bible and Tract Society. *The New World Translation of the Holy Scriptures: With References* (WTBTS, 1984).

_____ . "Questions from Readers," *The Watchtower* (Feb. 15, 1957): 126–27.

_____ . *"The Word"—Who Is He? According to John* (WTBTS, 1962).

# Index of Names

# Subject Index

Pages where terms are defined are italicized.

# Greek Words Index

# Hebrew Words Index

# Scripture Index

169